PURUSHAMEDHA

Lessons with His Holinesss
Sri Sankarsana das Goswami

PURUSHAMEDHA

ISBN-13: 978-0692510711

ISBN-10: 0692510710

© MARTINET PRESS 2015

MARTINET.PRESS@SAFE-MAIL.NET

All rights reserved. No part of this work may be reproduced in any way without the express permission of the publisher.

PURUSHAMEDHA

PURUSHAMEDHA

TABLE OF CONTENTS

INTRODUCTION	6
FIRESIDE CHAT	25
SATTVA, RAJAS, TAMAS	73
ON RAGANUGA BHAKTI	85
DISAPPEARANCE OF SANKARSANA DAS GOSWAMI	97
V IS FOR VAISNAVA	105
VAISNAVA HALLOWEEN?	111
SACRIFICE, THE VEDAS, & PRABHUPADA	115
CONTEMPORARY VEDIC WORSHIP AND SACRIFICE	119
THE PRACTICE OF INTERNAL WORSHIP	123
KNOWING THE GUNAS	127
UNLIMITED POWER	133
A MEDITATION ON RADHA FOR THE KALI YUGA	137
ASVAMEDHA	141
RUDRA DAS GOSWAMI (IMAGE)	155

INTRODUCTION

Hare Krsna! All glories to Sri Sankarsana das Thakur, whose teachings and devotion to Krsna are responsible for saving myself and others from a life of *maya* and illusion.

In 1985, I experienced a serious crisis of faith while studying for the priesthood. My family background was staunchly Roman Catholic and my parents had pushed me into seminary, where I was studying for the priesthood. My disposition had always been spiritual, and so it didn't seem like a bad fit – except I never really believed in the Church. I believed in a close and intimate God who calls all humanity into a personal experience, and there is a power to the holy sacraments and the holy orders that is tangible. When I'd take communion from my spiritual director, I would really feel the presence of God. But there was something that seemed missing, and I didn't have the words or the mental framework to describe it.

Then during one spring semester, the priest in charge of our Comparative Religion class began to invite guest speakers from different faith communities. So instead of just reading about Judaism and Islam, we had rabbis and imams explaining their faith, their beliefs and practices. They described their connection to the Supreme Being. It was a real eye-opener, since I have never genuinely imagined that other religions had any validity to them. Probably it sounds small-minded now, but back in the 80s, there just wasn't the same kind of religious pluralism or interfaith initiatives that you find today.

PURUSHAMEDHA

And then on one fateful day, our professor announced that the guest for that week would be a Hindu pandita. He was a jolly fellow, a Saivite, and a self-professed student of tantra. He didn't seem especially "priestly", and during his talk, he shared with us some rather compelling views on the failure of the Abrahamic theologies, and none of us (not even the teacher) could really argue with him. His explanation of dharma, karma, and samsara was really skillful, and the way he described his connection to the Supreme Being was genuinely moving. But what really attracted me were his stories of modern day Indian saints, who were so empowered that they were still capable of working the kinds of miracles that have entirely disappeared in the Christian tradition. These miracles, he explained, came from the science of bhakti (devotional) yoga.

When he finished class, I found myself in quandary. He clearly wasn't Catholic, but so much of what he'd said really hit home. I wanted to know more, and was afraid that if I didn't seize this chance, it might not appear again. So I asked if I could buy him dinner as thanks for the talk, and he graciously accepted. We agreed to meet the next evening at a local restaurant, and before he left the seminary classroom I found myself already compiling a list of questions to ask him over dinner.

Now the pandita was not a great saint by any means, and after meeting him for dinner, and later for coffee a few times, I realized that he just didn't have the answers I needed. He really tried to help me, to be fair, yet while he'd clearly seen some amazing things, he wasn't a very advanced tantric himself. On the bright side, though, he did have contacts back in India, and he promised that if I was genuinely interested in meeting some of the modern day saints (sadhus), he could arrange for me to stay with people who would introduce me to the types of guru that (he said) could answer my questions.

He did give one admonition which I won't forget: he said *Don't trust those so-called American Vaisnavas, those funny fellows who dress like Indians and shout and dance in public. They'll take your money and your sex-life and your career, and they'll make you give it all up, and they'll tell you it's for God. But that's not Vedic, and I know the Vedas well. That's not part of the Vedas or the Sashtras, and we don't allow that kind of nonsense in India. No real teacher will ever make you do that, so if you see those people, just avoid them. They're demons pretending to be saints, and no one needs lessons from a demon. Even your Satan can pretend to be an angel, and these people are pretending to be angels. So stay from those bad people, and go to India. Go to India, and you'll find the teacher you need.*

And I did. He said it with such sincerity and fervor that I went back to the seminary, telephoned my parents to ask for a loan, and arranged for a summer absence from my classes. Several weeks later, I was in Mumbai and beginning a journey that would lead me to a little place called Vrindavan.

India was a mind-blowing experience, or at least a mind-expanding experience. If you've never been there, it's really impossible to describe. Television and movies can show you the scenery, but India isn't just a visual experience. India is something that you taste, you feel, you inhale. Walking through streets where people have walked before you for three or four thousand years – wow! There's nothing like it. It's absolute chaos, but there's a strange order to the chaos, or at least a rhythm if not an order. Very quickly, you have to make a choice: are you a tourist or a traveler? A tourist is there just briefly, and makes no attempt to shed their foreign character. They're just passing through, snapping pictures and enjoying whatever Bollywood vacation package that they paid for. But the traveler enters India on its terms, and allows themselves to be absorbed into the amazing cultural matrix.

Now I was lucky: when I arrived in Vrindavan, an elderly friend of the pandita was expecting me and met me at the bus station. His name was Ramkrsna das, and he was a very friendly and hospitable person. He knew I was a student of religion, and so he treated me with a gentle (if humorous) respect that I certainly didn't feel worthy of at all. Although I tried to insist that I stay in a local guest house that the pandita recommended, Ramkrsna das insisted that I stay with his family. Not wanting to be a burden I tried to refuse, but hospitality is a very Indian virtue, and you can't refuse hospitality in Vrindavan. He was so delighted to have an American guest that he arranged for a yajna to be performed together with the sacrifice of a sheep, and at the time I did not realize how expensive that must have been to arrange. So from the beginning he was my host, and we soon became friends.

PURUSHAMEDHA

Now you can probably guess from the name: Ramkrsna das wasn't Saivite at all, he was a Gaudiya Vaisnava. His family, like the pandita's, was originally from the north, and he informed me that the pandita actually came from a Vaisnava family, but he'd fallen in with some tantric guru and become a worshipper of Lord Shiva. That happens all the time, of course – people worship whomever their guru worships, and I soon discovered that in many ways, the guru is the god (as the saying goes). And I heard many other stories about the pandita, which confirmed my suspicions that he was not at all a very religion man, but my time in seminary had certainly shown me that there are many Catholic priests who are hardly religious either, so this was hardly a shock. Ramkrsna das had a small home in the area of Govardhana hill, which was not a bad neighborhood in comparison. His wife, Radha devi dasi was a very handsome lady, and was a retired English teacher. Ramkrsna das had three children about my age, and all three had left home to begin their own families. I suppose having me there was a nice thing for them, as it occupied some days when otherwise the house might have been very empty. I remember that they had a very nice fireplace with some family photos - mostly smiling young adults (their kids), some older black-and-white photos of parents, and one recent photo (I guessed an uncle) who looked a little bit like a weathered version of Amitabh Bachchan.

Now it was early June when I arrived in Vrindavan, and Ramkrsna das spent most of the month taking me to see different teachers and gurus all over the region. He was retired and had a car, so we were able to drive some distance when need be. Ramkrsna das didn't know a lot of the gurus directly, but he knew people who knew other people who knew the gurus. Not every trip was pleasant – sometimes we drove an entire day, only to find the guru asleep or in Samadhi, and the trip was wasted. The trips around Vrindavan were much better, because the Vaisnavas there take hospitality so seriously that you were more likely to find helpful devotees who genuinely wanted to get you to meet the guru, and so I have better memories of those trips.

Let me confess: I have always had a serious weakness for religious architecture. Whether it's a temple or a church or a mosque, there is something truly profound about the way that a physical structure can affect the psyche. This is why, for example, Hinduism uses yantras and Buddhism has mandalas and Christianity has ikons – we try to make concrete the sacred – and so sacred buildings are really just a three-dimension effort to expand that initial sacred design which is originally just a two-dimension image.

So you can imagine how Vrindavan affected me. When you enter the Krsna-Balarama temple and feel the bhakti, or when you see the shaligram at Sri Radha Raman Mandir, it is hard not to begin weeping. My favorite temple in Vrindavan is and always will be Govindaji Temple, which was so beautifully made by the finest architects in the 16th century. You can see the red stone which the local devotees claim is from Acra, though Ramkrsna das tells me it's really from southern India, I really don't know the truth. My other favorite site is Rangaji Temple. It's not the biggest or the richest temple, but it has a beautiful murti of Lord Visnu reclining on the Sesha Naga. Ramkrsna das took me to all these places, of course, and somewhere in between the visits to the various holy places, I really fell in love with India, with Vrindavan, and with this new aspect of the Divine Person that I was beginning to discover.

Whatever his level of religiosity, the pandita hadn't been wrong about one thing: some of the different gurus really were amazing. One particular fellow struck me as especially odd for a spiritual leader. Ramkrsna das only referred to him as "Babaji", a *sadhu* or solitary hermit. He was a lean and hard man, deeply tanned and scraggly-bearded, and almost entirely naked except for what appeared to be a rag tied around his privates, and he was smeared with white paste. His eyes were dark and glinted brightly from his otherwise snowy face. When we arrived at his ashram, located on a river bank, he seemed entirely oblivious to his guests, but sat speaking with several other young devotees that seemed to emulate him in dress and appearance. Many of the other guests were Hindu, and they were really making a great show of obedience and humility to this strange mystic, who ignored them entirely. When he saw me, however, his eyes lit up and he stopped his talk momentarily. He pointed at me with a long, bony finger, and said something in Hindi that I couldn't understand at all. Then he laughed and laughed, and his students laughed too. Ramkrsna das smiled broadly and told me to greet the old sadhu, and so I bowed with folded palms. The sadhu seemed to approve, and motioned for me to approach. The crowd of visitors parted to let me through, and I hesitantly approached the naked holy man. This was definitely not something seminary had prepared me for! But the sadhu took my right hand, gently but firmly, and drew me to sit on the ground. He made a show of studying my face as if seeing deeply, and then put his right hand on my head (I cringed). He closed his eyes and intoned a phrase three times, and then nodded to Ramkrsna das. My friend thanked the sadhu, and I knew just enough Hindi to say *shukriya! Bahut shukriya, Maharaja* (thank you so much, your holiness!).

Once we were back in the car, I asked Ramkrsna das what had just happened. He congratulated me on what (he said) was a good visit. The old sadhu did not receive many foreigners, and when he saw me, he had declared: *Look, a demon* (asura) *comes! But I can help him, yes, I will help him*. Then the sadhu had blessed me (Ramkrsna das seemed to struggle with finding the right word), and removed some bad karmas from my path. As a Catholic student I should have been horrified, but I found myself deeply grateful to the kind old hermit.

Not all visits went as well. Many gurus are frauds, and there are a lot of people who put on the robes of monks and renunciates (*sannyasis*) for the wrong reasons. Ramkrsna das took me to several of the ISKCON temples, but he never stayed long and he kept me away from the saffron-clad Americans who were also travelers there. There was one very popular American sannyasi who was lecturing one Sunday when we were visiting Krsna-Balarama temple, and he was explaining about how sex and sexual desire (kama) were very dangerous for the devotees. His accent was New York for sure – I'm from Boston and I knew the difference to hear it. The American was tall and well-groomed, and I remember that he wore a very nice watch and he had a nice tan and expensive sun glasses. So I asked Ramkrsna das if we could sit with the guru, but he refused to go near him at all. This seemed perplexing since I would have guessed he'd want me to meet American followers of the dharma, but he'd shake his head and stop smiling when I asked about this. So I asked him what the problem was with us sitting with the American sannyasis. He looked thoughtful and said: "do you remember Babaji?"

I said yes, of course.

He said: "Babaji is a real sannyasi. He really has renounced everything, and now he lives on simple charity, tended to by a few poor students and some guests who bring gifts in hopes of his blessing. But this fellow (and he gestured at the American), he comes from some rich family in the US, he has a bank account and he arrived in a nice car. His students are wealthy. What has this man given up? I don't think he is a real renunciate, and if he were not a rich tourist, you know, he'd be run out of Vrindavan for this kind of vow-cheating."[1] He paused. "Besides, he's telling people

---

[1] And later, we were told that in a previous visit, the same American guru had been caught while soliciting a prostitute, but he was released by the authorities to avoid a scandal that would hurt tourism.

to stop having sex. Does he not know about the Kama Sutra? It's sashtra for householders! Jai Krsna, how stupid these fake monks can be."

So this gave me a certain wariness of Americans trying to "be" Hindu, though I learned later that dharma really has nothing to do with race, and that the hearts of those Americans were in the right place, just not in the right teacher.

The summer stretched into autumn, and I decided I should try to move out, so as to not tire out my welcome. But Ramkrsna das refused entirely to let me go, and swore that we would find my guru (as he would say) and not stop trying until the guru appeared. Then one morning, he spoke to me at breakfast, in a very serious tone. He said, "Son, you have been here now for several months, and I have tried to take you to all the gurus in the region – is it not so?" I acknowledged that it was certainly so. "Well then", he said slowly, "I think it may be time to take you to my gurudev."

What? This was new. Ramkrsna das was clearly a devout worshipper of Lord Visnu, but he'd never spoken about his own mentor. I was confused, and asked why we hadn't started with his own guru. He understood my confusion at once. "My gurudev has been travelling," he explained. "He just returned this week from Bengal, and he does not like to have many visitors. Besides," he added smiling slyly, "it would not be fair to the other gurus if you met my teacher first. He would have made the rest of them look bad."

Well, this was interesting. I confess, I hadn't been sure exactly how devout Ramkrsna's family was. On the one hand, he smoked sometimes and chewed betel, and we ate meat once or twice a week – it is expensive to get, and the family lived with moderate austerity. They had alcohol in the house, though I don't remember him ever drinking it while I stayed with them. So the idea of him having a guru was intriguing, especially because after being there for several months, I was hearing about him for the first time. Obviously, I asked to know more. So Ramkrsna das went to the mantle and got the photo of the uncle who looked like Amitabh Bachchan.

"This," he said proudly, "this is my gurudev, Sri Sankarsana das Thakur." He looked as though I should have recognized the name. When I continued to stare expectantly, he continued: "Sri Sankarsana is one of the few living disciples of Sri Lalita Prasad Thakur, the son of Bhaktivinoda Thakur."

Well, there was a name I did know from my textbooks. Bhaktivinoda Thakur was the great magistrate and scholar who had really revived the Vaisnava cause, and helped to bring the movement back into the prominence from which it had arguably fallen far in the Muslim period.

"But wait", I asked, "didn't Bhativinoda Thakur have only one son, Bimala Prasad Datta, and he founded the ISCKON movement that is so controversial?"

PURUSHAMEDHA

"No," Ramkrsna shook his head emphatically, "Old Bhaktivinoda had two sons. Black sheep and white sheep. You Catholics say Cain and Abel, well it's like that. He gave initiation to one son, Sri Lalita Prasad, but the other son, Bimala Prasad Datta, he was a bad rascal and started fights with other spiritual masters. He even attacked his father's guru, if you can imagine such an outrage. Anyway, they're both dead now, the two brothers. The bad son, he went against his father's wishes and introduced some very bad ideas into the Vaisnava movement. He wanted to make all the people sannyasi, but they didn't want that. So he redefined the householders to be *like* the sannyasi in almost every way, and then he gave the sannyasi the benefits of the householders."

"Is that why you don't speak to the American gurujis?" I asked.

"Yes exactly," he acknowledged, "Because they really have nothing in common with the old Vaisnava system that we still have here. Son, if you want to know more, you should really meet my guru. Sri Sankarsana studied with Sri Lalita Prasad Thakura, and he lives not too far from here, just outside Vrindavan."

Curious to meet this figure, I insistently asked when we could go to visit him. He agreed to take me to see the mysterious Sankarsana das in the morning, and I spent a relatively sleepless night tossing and turning, imagining what kind of guru Ramkrsna would think would make other gurus look bad.

PURUSHAMEDHA

In the morning we rose early, had breakfast, and headed out. The drive was more than an hour, of course, it was really closer to two hours altogether, and the road took us well outside of Vrindavan. I didn't recognize the particular route or any of the landmarks, and asked once or twice if we were lost. Ramkrsna just laughed and said, *maybe we are, but if Sankarsana wants you to come, no force on earth will keep you from going!* It was the typical kind of thing that Indians will say of their gurus, but I had never heard Ramkrsna express that kind of sentiment, and so it just fed my curiosity, making me want more and more to meet this particular old hermit.

Eventually our paved road became a little dirt road, often muddy and riddled with potholes, and it was hard for the car to get through. But the guru must have wanted us to come, because somehow the car kept moving and we didn't lose a tire. Finally we ended up at our destination: a little house, weathered and in need of a paint job. A few young men and women were in the yard outside tending to some goats and chickens – there were two girls (both British, I learned later) and three boys from Bengal. Ramkrsna das parked the car, and as he turned off the engine, I saw the door of the house open and a familiar figure stepped into the sunlight, squinting in our direction. I was surprised – I knew to expect from the photo of the distinguished looking guru, but I had somehow expected him to be more of a mendicant. All the sannyasis I had met wore robes and had shaved heads, where this fellow had very nice silver hair, and was dressed like any retired Bombay gentleman who was dressed to receive friends or visit a coffee house. He

PURUSHAMEDHA

said something in Hindi, and Ramkrsna das shouted something back. My host moved quickly to embrace his guru, and the older men embraced very warmly. I was surprised, since most gurus seemed to expect prostrations or pranams, where Ramkrsna das had embraced him like a brother or close friend. It was touching to see, and when they parted I could see Ramkrsna's eyes were wet with tears. This was a reaction he'd never had in visiting other gurus, even the few he knew personally and spoke well of. Ramkrsna took me by the arm and pulled me forward, so I was face to face with our host. "Maharaj," he said, "this is my American friend who has come all the way to see you. He has seen many bad gurus and a few good gurus, but maybe no real gurus, so I brought him to you." Then he turned to me and said, "This is my beloved guru-ji, Sankarsana das Goswami."

Sankarsana das reached out his hand to shake mine, and when I took his hand, his grip felt like iron. The aged sannyasi looked me in the eyes for a moment, and I noticed that he had very dark eyes which seemed to swallow all the light that shone around us – it was unnerving! He didn't say anything for what felt like a minute or two, and then suddenly he smiled. Then he spoke slowly in a deep voice, in good English, and said: *Look, a demon comes. But I can help him. Yes, I will help him.*

For the first time since I'd arrived in India, I felt something *shift* in my chest. There was a rushing sound in my ears, and my vision blurred. His grip tightened on my hand, and he kept me from falling. For a moment, it was not the old guru standing before me, but rather that naked sadhu on the riverbank. What was happening to me? Then I felt Ramkrsna das put his arms around me and help me towards the doorway of the little house, and the two men speaking in Hindi in low voices. The world was just spinning, and everything in front of my eyes was very dark. Then someone was putting a glass into my hands and saying "here, drink, drink". I tasted cool milk, and the spinning began to subside. When I came to, I was sitting on a low bench in a small dim salon – clean if poor – and the two older men were looking at me with concern. *Are you feeling better?* asked Ramkrsna das kindly. I assured them that I was, and I must have gotten too much sun. When I said that, Sankarsana laughed (not unkindly) and I noticed that the room was not so much dim as it just could not seem to hold any light around him. It was really unnerving – I'd seen nothing like it since I arrived. Then before I could speak, Ramkrsna das rose to his feet, and began to head for the door.

"Where are you going?" I cried.

"Oh, I brought you where you're supposed to be," he assured me, "I'll be back in a few days, and you can decide then if you are staying or going."

Sankarsana das said nothing, watching me carefully. Part of me wanted to get out of that dark little salon and get back in the car, but another part of me somehow knew – KNEW – that this man was why I'd come to India. This man was my only chance to get real answers, or to get help, as he called it.

So I bid Ramkrsna das goodbye, at least for a few days. And when he returned a week later, he was not surprised at all when I told him I'd be staying and studying with Sankarsana das Goswami. During that first week, I learned more about myself, my karmas, my dharma, and the world in general, than I had learned in several years at seminary. More importantly, in that first week, Sankarsana showed me real miracles. Some of them were states of mind, but others were the real thing – I mean miracles like you read about in the Bible or the Vedas. So I became his disciple, and he became my guru. It was the best decision of my life, and I have never looked back. For nearly thirty years, Sri Sankarsana served as my mentor, my father, and my best friend. During that time I travelled with him throughout India, though most of the time we were always near Vrindavan.

Sri Sankarsana das Goswami taught me the sashtra. I don't mean the Vedic literatures alone, but the Vedas themselves. Sri Sankarsana helped to explain the sashtra – not merely repeating the conventional fables that so many modern gurus have invented, but he really helped me to understand how the Dharma had changed over the past thousand years. Much of what he taught would have horrified the modern, puritanical Indians – and it did horrify a lot of the international "gurus" who tried to argue with him – but his knowledge of sashtra and the commentaries was encyclopedic. He helped me to see the Indian religions not just in the current post-Muslim form, but also in their original form from before the Mughal period. He made the Vedas come alive. Most importantly, he taught me Krsna – and he taught me to love Krsna.

In 2013 my gurudev disappeared, leaving behind a ragged collection of disciples. At first, we didn't know what to do. Our guru had only just given us permission to begin sharing his teachings – before he had refused, because he was such a private man. But when he disappeared, what next? Over the last two years, my godbrothers and godsisters have worked to recall and to recite his most important lessons. We have forgotten too much already, but the most important talks we have written here, in hopes that it may be of help to other young Vaisnavas all over the world.

This book might offend you. In fact, if you're a Vaisnava from any of the international preaching missions, it will definitely offend you. Please accept my apologies for that in advance. But the purpose of this book is not merely to offend you, but rather to tear the bandage off your eyes. Sankarsana would say sometimes: You have been lied to, and you are lying to yourself. He wasn't wrong. Most modern spiritual leaders are frauds – and with increased media and internet, we're aware of their many, many failings. So if you worship your guru, and your guru is a fraud, this book will offend you. But sometimes offence is good. We are too sanitized, too protected, too afraid to ruffle feathers. Sankarsana used to say: *see Krsna, what a little rascal! What does he do? He steals food. He kills his uncle Kamsa. He fucks pretty girls. He even fucks the pretty*

PURUSHAMEDHA

married girls – eh, Radha? Is Krsna worried about offending you? No, so I won't be afraid to offend you either! Krsna is a fiend. And we need to be fiends, just like him. When he would say this to American sannyasis who came to visit, some of them would get violent. Most of them would sputter references to Lord Caitanya, but Sankarsana would say: *Caitanya was quite a trickster, like Lord Buddha! What, you don't quote Lord Buddha, eh? Well then don't quote Caitanya to me – quote Vedas instead, since we agree on the Vedas.* And of course, no sannyasis today even know a verse of the Vedas, whereas Sankarsana had memorized most of them and could quote them at length. So those arguments usually ended the same way – some offended sannyasi leaving in a huff. But sometimes, rarely but sometimes, someone else would feel the room spinning, and see the light draining out of the room. Then Sankarsana das would get another disciple, and if they didn't always stay as long as me, they took some of his transcendental energy away with them when they went.

My prayer for you, as you read this book, is that you'll be offended. I want you to be shocked, and to get angry. Because if you're being complacent in your devotion to Krsna, then you have no passion, and no love of Krsna. If you worship your guru, then you don't really worship Krsna. My guru always said *Don't worship me! I'm just a shadow. You can't worship me and Krsna. So love me, but worship Krsna.* And I tell you the same thing: **love Krsna**. That's all that matters. Krsna is really a sociopathic monster, but he loves you. And he will do things to you – horrible things – because he loves you. Krsna is the abusive and jealous boyfriend or girlfriend that you can't escape. He has your email passwords and your phone contacts and he is watching your every move. You can never get free of Krsna, but you can learn to love Him. When He is hurting you, and beating you until you bleed and are screaming for Him to stop, that is when you need to love Him the most.

These words might offend you, but once you really start to Love Krsna, you will see that it's true. So please, read this book. Read the words of my guru, Sri Sankarsana das Goswami. If you're feeling a little bit uncomfortable, I'm sorry. It's going to get worse. Because Krsna isn't a comfortable god. Far from it. But this is my promise to you: if you stick with me on this journey – if you read every word – you will never see Krsna the same. Sankarsana das will open your eyes, your ears, and other senses you didn't even know you had.

(*You don't need eyes to see where we're going*, he'd say).

For any errors in spelling or typing, forgive me. My guru deserves better than me as an editor. But I will do my best to write, and if you do your best to read, I think we'll get there. In the end, it's not the journey that matters. It's Krsna that matters, and if we're sincere about reaching him, then we'll get there no matter what.

Ready? Good. Hang on tight – this is going to be a rocky ride.

- Rudra das Goswami.

PURUSHAMEDHA
FIRESIDE CHAT

I have been a disciple of His Holiness Rudra dasa Goswami for over ten years now and for each and every one of them and every one yet to come in this life and the next I thank Sri Guru for leading me out of the ocean of base material bondage and beyond the normal human confines of good and evil - both of which can only be realized through genuine transcendence - and for placing me on the iron-clad frigate of Krsna Consciousness through which all living entities can experience true rapture and untold bliss through the chanting of the following mantra:

Hare Krsna Hare Krsna
Krsna Krsna Hare Hare
Hare Rama Hare Rama
Rama Rama Hare Hare

My name is Kumbhakarna dasa, which is a name that doesn't necessarily ingratiate me with most devotees in North India - except for a few small provincial villages where the import matches the sampradaya orientation (increasingly rare however - even the Tantrics are sometimes, actually most of the times appalled, but that rasa we can enjoy - ha!).

As such, when in Vrindavan and the surrounding regions in Uttar Pradesh, when in Bengal and also out and about where people would take particularly negative notice we go by our English name - Keith - or in communities of devotees not of my specific matha, Karna, which is still somewhat questionable - but not nearly to the same degree.

My name is not indicative of an ordinary Vaisnava (and as a caveat there is no such thing as an "ordinary" Vaisnava - for everyone Vaisnava is extraordinary) and if you were to meet me (and many of you have) you would not immediately think of me in the context of an archetypal "Hare Krsna", bell-tinkling and flower-selling someone-or-other on the side of a random metropolitan street (though I do that on occasion - and everyone buys a flower, when pressed).

The body I possess is very large, Krsna's "little" gift to an otherwise putrid existence (and irony here, because any existence whether in heaven or hell if serving Krsna is relishable) and with an ample profusion of reddish hair both on face and head.

When I first encountered Maharaja I was engaged in semi-professional power-lifting meets and it was outside of a rather grimy establishment in south Boston ("Southie" to you lesser Yankees) where I first encountered him and a handful of his disciples. After hours of preparation in the squalid gym followed by fifteen minutes of being slapped in the face and screamed at by sweating fat men and a few passable native broads and multiple inhalations of (insert power-lifting enhancing inhalant of choice) I had bested my previous bench - raw category - with the guttural sounds of death metal blaring from the ailing PA system that the gym owners has "rented" for the occasion.

PURUSHAMEDHA

While I hadn't won the meet - and barely qualified for the upcoming event - I was happier than the figurative pig in shit for besting my then personal best. The Miller flowed and with about the ninth or tenth can in less than an hour I exited the service doors in a particularly hale and hearty mood - a somewhat crumpled can of suds cupped in one hand and a pile of stinking wraps, straps and other sundry accessories contained within a freebie gym bag in the other.

The disqualified had already left, in something of a huff, and the gym owner and his personal friends, some of those newly minted (all of which included those who had benched, squatted and dead-lifted poundage decidedly higher than me) were still in the gym and probably would be until two or three o'clock in the morning, if previous records for post-meet partying set a general rule for precedence.

I had an early shift scheduled for the next morning - dock security as the case may be (I am now, with Krsna's blessings, employed in private force protection here and abroad) - so I had decided to cut-out early. Plus that, the usual shenanigans that were happening on the other side of the gym doors were those that I had experienced to a surplus degree - to wit, I had had my fill. No great existential crisis of any sort, but the culture - which I very much enjoyed - had its limits. Double-plus that, a good night's sleep was the veritable salve to the soul of muscle - and I was already a few sheets clear of sobriety, all the better that my apartment was within walking distance.

PURUSHAMEDHA

With nothing but the clean feel of a qualifying push-press driven victory behind me and the not-so-clear elation of a gut full of suds - all the more fluid for the creatine to transmit I thought to myself, in predictably drunken reasoning, I exited the gym and turned the corner onto the several-block walk only to be met with a more than somewhat strange sight, for me, which careened into a very strange experience of which I have never extricated myself (and Krsna willing, never will).

At first I thought that I had suddenly run into an impromptu gathering of puny neo-nazi skinheads - for most of them were puny in the comparative sense that they didn't seem to be dosed with (insert weekend-warrior illegal anabolic supplement of choice) and by the fact that we, as such, towered over them to a ridiculous degree in the physical sense.

The second thing that struck me as odd was that, while wearing street clothes passably salient to the era and to the weather (the second especially important in Boston) everything seemed completely disjointed. Their attire reminded me of how the wizards appeared sometimes in the "Harry Potter" book series - how they wore "human" clothes only in cases of attempted coversion and then so barely passing normative standard - being more used to wearing the flowing robes of "their kind" (and this latter similarity in fact was, as it turned out, completely on the money). More than a few pairs of mismatched socks and a few shirts that barely qualified for that designation, appearing as if they had randomly grabbed items from a discount bin at the local thrift store so as not to have to appear on the street naked, only strengthened the comparative notion in my mind.

As they turned their attention on me, most of them smiling in that particular fashion which is known to some in modern Vaisnava parlance as being "blissed out", one other wearing a slight beard and looking definitely sly, a young sylph of a girl ran out from amidst their number and promptly jumped directly toward me, curling her legs around my midsection and arms around my chest before planting a big sloppy kiss right on the side of my unshaven cheek.

Due to the fact that both hands were occupied (the Miller can slightly more crumpled and now damn near empty) and the fact that the girl, who couldn't have been more than twelve or thirteen, looked every inch like a young Brooke Shields - except that she was dressed in a strange ensemble of silken headdress, and flowing garments (what I learned later was that northern Indian garment known as a "Punjabi suit") and had a strange yellowish marking going from the middle of her nose up toward the top of her head - left me in a somewhat flustered state.

If the girl had flung herself at one of the other assembled devotees with that degree of velocity they would have assuredly fallen over but, luckily for her, she was able to cling to my frame briefly for her brief ministrations before she slid off and winked once before running off, laughing. Amply surprised and somewhat embarrassed I drank the last dregs from my can before tossing it aside and the sly man with the beard shouted "Gopi-bhava!" with an undisguised sense of delight to which his shaven-headed compatriots laughed heartily, the girl giggled and I simply turned a deeper shade of red, having no clue then as to the import of the "insider" joke.

After the fact, introductions were made all around and despite all, my curiosity overcame my need for a somewhat early start for work the next morning (I had the overwhelming urge to call in sick after the fact but didn't, as the fresh cold wind off the water and the inevitable lulls in the security detail there at the docks allowed me ample time to consider and reflect on the night before and to read some of the literature that the devotees had left with me before our parting).

We made our way a few blocks further in the direction of my apartment before stopping at an Irish pub which as the time was not yet eleven was just getting started, so we were able to procure a large circular corner booth. Several of the men didn't imbibe, a fact to which the barkeep was decidedly nonplussed as he served them cups of water and there were no ladies present other than the young look-a-like Miss Shields, who was served a Shirley Temple on the house, much to the amusement of the sly one with the small beard.

That one however - who I later took initiation from and who is none other than my spiritual master, His Holiness Rudra dasa Goswami - set himself up with a bottle of Jameson's and a glass and proceeded to drink more neat whiskey in a sitting than I had witnessed for some time. The Catholic priests from the neighborhood liked to come in for a tipple (or two, or three and sometimes, ad nauseam - though their parishioners pretended not to notice too much) now and again, but for a holy man, this was ridiculous.

And the thing is - the kicker - is that the guy didn't seem to get drunk - not one little bit. Sure, he was witty, his conversational skills much more sophisticated and more humorous, even while elucidating very deep spiritual concepts and scathing social commentary - but he was completely on point, not one chink in his armor as he quaffed the stuff, no deterioration no matter how much alcohol he put down. The mischievous twinkling in his eyes was there before he came into the pub and was there after - his baseline - which I now know was his inherent spiritual potency shining through.

I continued drinking Miller - Miller low-life, as my father liked to call it - but my pacing slowed considerably in comparison to the rapidity of my drinking back at the power-lifting meet. Alot of what RDG and the devotees said I didn't readily understand at the time, but it got me to thinking - some very deep thinking in fact, deeper than I had thought it seemed during my entire lifetime.

After a few more weeks at the docks and as many meetings with my soon to be spiritual master and his disciples my mind was made up - I put in my notice and told my friends at the gym, who were only passingly sorry to see me go and headed south to an incipient farm community (which ultimately failed) farther than far from my usual haunts and equally culturally uncomfortable, way down there in the cotton-laden land of Alabama.

The time in Alabama went by with a whirlwind of activity and although the venture ultimately ended in failure at least according to concrete standards (we ended up - after a few years - selling the land at a loss and moving on, much to the appreciation of the vast majority of the local populace) it provided a heated atmosphere of ordeal and spiritual development for all the devotees involved. My spiritual master was only present for a few weeks a year, but those were the highlights for all of us during which everything seemed to coalesce on a spiritual level and made our erstwhile efforts worth the while.

It was there in Alabama where I was given initiation and also where my spiritual master received the inspiration for my name, which is a story in and of itself.

During the time at the farm - which was little more than a semi-pentagon collection of run-down trailer homes in deep need of repair - and a farm only in the most titular sense, as none of the crew, most of us from Boston, knew a damn thing about eking out an existence from the unyielding red clay. Thus, in probably the most unyielding ground for amateur farming in all of Alabama and within a community as equally or more unyielding in their hostility to our presence we spent our days sweating, plying our shovels into the dirt, chanting like our life depended on it (and it did) and engaging in multiple political maneuverings against entrenched natives who made it their life's work to make our lives a living hell.

While in Alabama the senior devotees - including a couple of Dravidians from brahmin families - whose ebony dark complexions irked the locals more than you can imagine - instituted the time-honored practice of mangala-aarati - with all in attendance - starting at the ungodly hour of 4:30 A.M. (which required waking at least a half-hour before in order to apply tilak, shit-shower-and-shave, etc).. Since I was still lifting - though not in meets at the time - the power-lifting scene in that part of Alabama all but nonexistent - and driving an hour and a half both ways to a gym five days out of seven - the schedule was more arduous for me than some of the others. In effect, most of the time I was M.I.A. - and as the other devotees increasingly realized over time that it was a waste of their time trying to wake me up, I remained asleep. The sounds of the clanging kirtans echoing across the hot mornings from the other trailer that served as the temple room were going straight to my subconscious nonetheless.

There were exceptions to this schedule however and they usually occurred when my spiritual master arrived from whatever obscure corner of the world he had been visiting - whether for preaching, meditation or god only knows whatever more nefarious purposes I can only imagine. He kept his schedule secret most of the time and would appear unbidden at homes or small centers maintained by his disciples across the globe and if he did clue them in to his visit he would usually arrive several days later or several days earlier than the time he had specified to his disciples. Not yet involved in the more pointy side of the security business, but having an instinctive propensity in that direction, I assumed that he believed his phone was tapped and that he may have been shadowed by some sort of investigative police element - thus the secrecy and inconsistent arrivals and departures (the latter which were almost never announced). All more proof positive that my guru maharaja is a very, very interesting fellow.

On some of these visits there would be a Kali-puja, at midnight, as tradition dictates. These would - as tradition dictates but which is seldom followed in the west, mostly for purposes of legality - with a sacrificial conclusion. Where the animals would be procured will be specified later in the story but sufficient it to say, the risks were somewhat lessened by the relative isolation of our compound and the fact that this operating base of the matha was situated in an agrarian area - though if any locals had reported what went on during those midnight gatherings the state police would have been all over our tract of mortgaged land as quick as you could say Lynyrd Skynyrd.

I was present for most of these, at least in part, but sometimes I would arrive around mid-way during the long drive back from the gym and quietly park my aging Gremlin on the outer edge of the field by the road and make my way back to the residential mobile home which served as the asrama/living quarters and collapse onto the mattress and then very soon into sleep, while hearing the sounds of rapidly chanted Sanskrit mantras executed by RDG and the south Indian brahmins and the tinkling of the offering bells as I drifted into pleasantly uneasy dreams.

On these occasions however - in distinction to my usual morning routine (which was to wake as I damned well pleased - and challenge to the brahmacari who attempted to get too enthusiastic about waking me, godbrother or no - he would regret it) I always seemed to rouse, pleasurably in fact, right around the time that mangala-arati would be getting started - in those magic pre-dawn hours when the apsaras played and the beaming face of Brahma shone down upon the earthlings with all due benevolence (or so I was told).

The factor was the meat.

After the Kali-puja RDG and his immediate attendants would retire and the remains of the sacrificed animals would be transferred to a few brahmacaris who would dress the meat and after due preparation lay it out on the big smoker which they had made just for such occasions out of an old farmhouse water reservoir that they had picked up at the scrapyard in town for a song. Right around four in the morning - after several hours of low and slow - the smell of that meat would start wafting through the screen window which was always kept open in my room, with a small box fan rigged for intake (as a large man and also a one-hundred-and-ten percent Bostonian in this life, the window was open and fan going whatever the weather during my tenure in the south) and a smile would begin to involuntarily cross my face and waking, soon thereafter. Once awake - laziness not being a cultivated trait - and in premeditation of a more opulent breakfast prasadam than usual after managala-arati - I would adorn myself with tilak with all the appropriate mantras, don a dhoti (my spiritual master insisted I wear white rather than the saffron of the brahmacaris, not trusting my abilities at celibacy) and head into the trailer that served as the temple room and make good on the morning program with as much zeal as the more zealous early risers among our number.

Needless to say, this marked disparity in my attendance record at the morning program was quickly noticed among the community of my godbrothers and godsisters and not surprisingly began to become an inside joke (which I was woefully unaware of most of the time) which filtered its way up to His Holiness Rudra dasa Goswami.

The culmination of all this came one early dark Spring morning after a Kali-puja during one of RDG's visits.

Predictably and true to form I began to wake with a smile, my eyes still closed for a few moments as I relished the upcoming "pastimes" (working up a sweat during kirtan but more importantly to my mind, that succulent slow-roasted pork for which I would be the first in line).

Before my eyes opened naturally I heard a damn near inhuman scream from less than two feet from my face and then words booming with a theatrical bass inflection:

PURUSHAMEDHA

"Rise O Brother, O Greatest among the Rakshashas!"

What happened next was more embarrassing than some of the previous incidents I have relayed but for you, the reader, I will indulge your amusement at my expense.

Around four of the brahmacaris pinioned me down (with no small difficulty mind you - despite the shock of being wakened suddenly and not possessed of my full faculties after less than my usual mandatory ten hours in the sack) while another attempted to pour the nectar from the bathing of the deities (a combination of tirtha water, ghee, yogurt and other assorted ingredients) into my mouth.

The person doing the pouring with the lota was first to get it. Enraged, I slammed out with as much force was possible in a prone position and swept his feet out from under him. The lota, still half-full of nectar, flew across the room and bonked with a less than resounding thud against the faux wood-paneled wall.

The two brahmacaris attempting to restrain my upper body were the next to get it as I flung myself upward from the waist with all the force I was able to muster. Having a decided weight advantage, they too toppled aside but not before I began wailing wildly with balled fists, attempting to injure any bodily form in my immediate vicinity as I let out a roar of outraged protest at this most ignominious wakening.

I only desisted when I spotted across the room my spiritual

master - doubled-over with laughter. Hazing was a fact of life in any environment where more men than women congregated in close quarters, but this was pushing it. Despite that fact, my inherent reverence for maharaja and the inconceivable spiritual potency which emanated from him even in the moments of utmost levity calmed my jets.

Regaining his bearings amidst his mirth, Rudra dasa Goswami stood at full height - his face beaming a smile like a soothing Vrindavana moon - his eyes wet with tears - before stating with all authority: "Your name is now Kumbhakarna dasa!"

RDG initiated me that very morning.

After mangala-arati and class, during which he had a few godsisters scrambling on another part of the compound to gather all the necessary puja items for an impromptu initiation yajna, he took us all out to the section of grounds shielded from the seldom-trafficked road by the catty-corners of two adjoining trailers.

There he instructed me to remove my shirt, leaving me bare-chested as he began to spoon ghee into the sacrificial fire while intoning various mantras.

A godbrother approached me from behind as I sat and removed my tulasi neck beads, affixing a new set - three strands rather than one - about my neck.

PURUSHAMEDHA

PURUSHAMEDHA

My spiritual master gave a brief lecture - the details of which I regrettably cannot remember except that they dealt with transcendental matters which were addressed toward all of the assembled devotees but which were specifically aimed for my hearing. Although I cannot - or choose not - to recall the details via this medium, the import of his initiation lecture via auspices most occult have become the linchpin of every tactic and strategy which I have employed in Krsna's service ever since.

After less than fifteen minutes he gestured for me to come forward and I did so, giving full obeisances on the cold wet ground (for it was still early Spring and the dew still saturated the seldom-mowed grass, as the sun was not yet fully risen upon the horizon).

He gave me my beads - a huge maha-maha tulasi mala dark from soaking in oil - and pronounced my name.

"You are now - Kumbhakarna dasa!"

All the devotees let out a roar of approval.

After that he gave a brief summation about my name - indicating that while Kumbhakarna was in titular sense an asura, he was actually a great devotee of Lord Visnu in Vaikunthaloka - a security guard, no doubt, who guarded the gates of the innermost sanctum of the Vaikuntha planets.

During one occasion in time before reckoning - a situation

cunningly engineered by Visnu Himself - the devotee who would later be known as Kumbhakarna in the treta-yuga and his brother offended a visiting sage. Because of this offense, the two brothers were cursed to take birth on the earth planet and become demons. Maharaja explained however that although this curse was the apparent reason for the brothers descent to the earth and rebirth as demons that actually it was the greatest boon, for Visnu was facilitating these brothers to please him in his earthly pastimes by performing the necessary but thankless task of becoming His worthy opponents and assisting him in a most quintessential way for the enactment of his pastimes.

After the initiation I and the other devotees feasted on the remnants of the Kali-puja from the night before. The other devotees jokingly tried to push me to the back of the line and my spiritual master loudly announced that it was the duty of the newly minted initiate to clean up the ritual accoutrements of the initiation yajna.

Humbly, but with a discernible sense of petulance I acquiesced, before RDG and the other devotees laughed and led me to the large fold-out table where the pork had been pulled and seasoned - a prodigious plate already prepared for me, with all the fixings and ample enough for a demon's consumption, which was promptly shoved into my hands.

Not intending to disappoint, I ate the entire thing.

Events there at the Alabama property turned distinctly

darker after my initiation leading up to the eventual breaking of our fellowship (at least in a temporal sense) - though not one of the residents complained and every one of us considered it to be Krsna's blessing that we could suffer and, in turn, make others suffer, in His transcendental service.

The conflicts with the local residents had begun almost as soon as we had arrived. The sale of the property had been done remotely, through a proxy buyer (RDG's lawyer) as the contract signatory and as the truth had been amply bent or more correctly obscured as to both the actual identity of the purchaser and the reason for the procurement of the real-estate the seller felt betrayed, which was the first drop of poison in the well. While ethically questionable according to backwoods standards (though no doubt that the good old boy network of land barons in the area probably did much worse on a regular basis - pot, kettle, black) the contract had integrity as to the letter of the law so there was nothing that could be done about our residency except to apply pressure in other ways.

As such, maneuvering around obtaining basic supplies and doing day-to-day business in the immediate town became something of a headache. So to avoid this, the devotees started taking their business to the nearest town of a decent size which was where my gym was located, though the city (in name only, not population classification) was less than the size of some of the smaller boroughs surrounding my native Boston.

PURUSHAMEDHA

While well past being a staging ground for the "white hate" counter-intel operations of the investigative branch of the federal government there was still a lingering distaste for foreigners (up to and including fellow countrymen from north of that invisible but ever-present Mason-Dixon line). And for out-and-out exotic foreigners - such as the our two-resident brahmins (down-home boys from Thiruvananthapuram and Malappuram respectively) outright howling indignity.

In the defense of the town-folk, it does go with remarking that my godbrothers from Kerala did little to nothing to ingratiate themselves with anyone (including some of their godbrothers and godsisters, truth be told) and as to sinews softening in that melting pot that is America they were every-inch hardboiled and indigestible - no compromise. They dressed in flowing south Indian style dhotis with decorative borders all of the time - the thought of attempting to blend in even to the slightest degree not even a notion on the back end of a notion. The first time one of my godsisters and I took them to the nearest grocery store (a Piggly Wiggly) to procure some items for a puja which they did not feel they could entrust us with purchasing on our own recognizance they attempted to haggle with the cashier. I managed to stifle my laughter with a fist against my mouth, my godsister turned red as an apple and giggled quietly to herself, gaze toward the floor and the aging lady cashier looked like she had just been slapped.

The local bar was one point of contention - though the only reason any of the devotees went into the place was that it was really the closest thing to a gas station slash mini-mart in the immediate area, excepting the gas pumps out in front of the mechanic's which were utilized from time to time (and if at all possible gas was purchased further afield). The actual nearest proper bar was well further down the highway and very rurally situated - Boondocker's at the County Line - so named because it was in (obvious guess here) the boondocks and secondly because it straddled the line between the semi-populated county where the devotees lived and another adjoining county which was even less populated, dedicated almost solely to commercial hunting retreats and agriculture.

But the bar that became a flashpoint for the other devotees and I was a bar only in the most nominal sense - it was what the country folk called a "beer bar" (no spirits served) and further even than that, a "bottle bar" only (everything stored in one aging cooler, bottles and cans - no kegs, no taps, no glasses). This part of the establishment was literally only a small corner in the store where three little tables and chairs were set and a few stools on the far-end of the cashier's counter where the local farmers would sit and tie one on during the twilight hours and later, if the proprietor took it into his heart to join them past usual closing hours. But, as is well known to anyone who has experienced the sometimes extreme behavior of people under the influence where "particular people congregate" it attracted as much trouble as a full-blown nightclub (in a microcosmic sense, at least) and as it so happened - as the decidedly outsider element in the area - the devotees were the focal point for trouble.

PURUSHAMEDHA

You would think that the devotees at our compound wouldn't want to visit a place where alcohol was served, though if you have paid attention to the general thrust of my spiritual master's branch of the sampradaya thus far you probably know better by now. Some of the devotees were somewhat abashed - for that esoteric reason which no one outside of the devotee community would ever suspect - namely that places where alcohol was served were drawing points for ghosts and spirits, said ghosts and spirits who proceeded to affect the consciousness of those inhabiting such places in a myriad of negative ways. Being ultimately compassionate however, the godbrothers (and the godsisters especially) believed that the Holy Name should be spread to such unfortunate living entities - all creatures great and small (even those without physical bodies) so as a few of us shopped usually a few more of our number would wander through the aisles, hands in beadbags, muttering the mahamantra under their breath and watching for the potential of some supernatural conversion experience. I found it all very humorous at first, but in time the cumulative effect became no laughing matter (except perhaps for Krsna - that grandest amongst sociopaths).

On the first several occasions there was small, low-level attempts at provocation on behalf of the locals when we were in the store. Snickering loudly as to let us know that they were, especially when the always robed Keralite bramhims were present - though the looks that they returned to the few drunken rednecks was capable of curdling milk, them dirt-covered from a day of toil and the brahmins resplendent in silken dhotis and fiery eyes shining out from faces near-black with pure Dravidian racial complexion.

There were also ministrations made toward the godsisters - catcalling and that sort of thing - to which there was apparently no reaction in response that didn't add fuel to the fire. A few of the godsisters, imperious as queens, responded by ignoring their would-be suitors - proffering nothing than a look in response of the greatest disdain before going about their chanting. Others would attempt to engage the few drunks - a chink in the armor to exploit as a preaching opportunity, so went their reasoning - and those incidents usually ended somewhat disastrously.

It is outside of the scope of this essay to mention everything that led up to our leaving Alabama and as some of the incidents would impinge on the privacy of several parties with even barest description such have been omitted.

There ended up being one fight outside of the station - myself primarily included insofar as participation from the devotee community - and from there, as is often the case in these type of scenarios especially in rural areas where conflict can be nurtured intensively for lack of other distracting stimulus, the situation turned into a gradual but increasingly dangerous game of one-upmanship by both parties.

All of this came to a head one week less than six months since my taking initiation when everyone at the community was in a low-ebb of morale for various reasons. RDG hadn't been to visit us in as many months and, close-mouthed as ever excepting a few general letters that were read out during the morning program and brief but expensive long-distance telephone calls with the senior devotees who handled the administrative side of things, everyone had basically been left to fend for themselves spiritually - which I think may have been intentional on the part of my spiritual master. The farming - or the attempt at it - was proving to be a miserable failure, despite the long hours of arduous yet apparently inept labor that everyone had done out in the fields. In this, in retrospect, I can very much commiserate with the sort of experiences that the old communes (whatever their ideological stripe) may have gone through back in the sixties when you took city folk without practical knowledge of the land who, while well-meaning, were in far out of their depth and had bitten off more than they could chew.

In an effort to raise the spirits of the devotee community in the face of ever-increasing tension coming from outside it was decided that a Kali-puja would be arranged administered directly by the devotees on-site - which is something that we hadn't previously done excepting during the visits of RDG when he would provide his services as general manager of the proceedings. Everyone, myself included, wanted to make this one special and in the immediate the idea seemed to play into the intention of those who had broached the idea in the first place - morale seemed to be raised. Even the south Indian brahmins, who could be notoriously grumpy, seemed to brighten to the notion.

PURUSHAMEDHA

It was the brahmins who had the idea that we should not only do a Kali-puja alone but also do pujas to some of the even nastier and more obscure wrathful goddesses of their native region. One of the priests was half-Tamil and he had several names to put forward as to appropriate objects of veneration. Seemingly crude (from a Western perspective) altars were arranged for various of these wrathful goddesses but elaborately decorated with all manner of colored powders, garlanded with limes and surrounded with large aarathi lamps that the brahmins only brought out on occasion. Though not anthropomorphic, the central part of the shrines were not entirely aniconistic as the brahmins had drawn terrible faces on them - and the descriptions that they cheerfully gave the rest of the devotees were even more terrifying in import.

During this period leading up to the pujas a sense of unreality seemed to permeate the entire area of our little compound and it was the general feeling amongst all of the Vaisnavas and Vaisnavis that we were taking place in a divine lila, a pastime of reciprocation with the Supreme Being, Krsna, while on earth - just as the intimate associates of Krsna did five-thousand years ago at the very end of the Dvarpa-yuga. In these lilas, conflict with the outside - with those whom Krsna had deemed to act as his adversaries - while oftentimes horrifying for the devotees, only served to increase Krsna's pleasure as the supreme enjoyer.

During the small hours of morning various devotees who shall remain nameless for various reasons began to make forays into some of the local farms and steal livestock for the pujas. Mostly brahmacaris acting in small cells of two to three persons, there ended up being an increasing sense of competition among them and often fueled with alcohol some of these forays began to get reckless. The ultimate example of recklessness in this regard was perpetrated by none other than some of my godbrothers who were also fellow neighborhood boys from Southie who decided to cull an animal on the spot and, with some of their questionable blue-collar skills (including butchery, as one of them had been born into the profession) from years back in New England, decided to make one such culling resemble a "cattle mutilation" with a little creative cutting here, a bit of cauterization there and organ removal.

Ultimately the planned Kali-puja - and puja of the associated deities, planned on the traditional date congruent to the event in Bengal which is tantamount to a national holiday there, never occurred. The Boston brahmacaris who had decided to go beyond due measure in their enthusiastic forays into neighboring farms had crossed the line for all of us, though they only admitted to a few after the fact what they had done. Soon thereafter, a day or so before the puja was scheduled, one of our administration people received a phone call - apparently from RDG - who had heard that a police raid on the commune was imminent with instructions for us to get out post-haste.

I was one of the first to go having my own vehicle and having no wish to dally. I know that some of the other devotees at the time felt my enthusiasm in cutting out as quickly as I did seemed traitorous for whatever reason, and

I hope that by now they have forgiven me. Those that tarried too late and may have gotten caught up in the net in one way or the other, on the other hand, probably wished that they had emulated my own exit strategy.

I packed a few of the more egregious perpetrators stuffed into the back of the Gremlin along with my meager personal belongings and had them hunker down to the floorboards until we were well across the county line, so for all effective purposes for those that may have been watching (and I was almost certain there were people watching especially at the junction near the turn-off for the commune) it would appear that I was out for my usual foray to the gym. As the case was, I didn't find myself in a gym again until more than a week later - back in Boston.

The raid happened on the night that the Kali-puja was to have taken place - a joint operation by the local Sheriff's Department and State Police even with a few SBI agents in tow. By this point many of the locals (some of the farmers who had bore the brunt of my godbrothers' excesses especially) would have loved to take part as an extra-legal posse but even back then the state police involvement was enough to stymie that type of volunteerism (though if the warrant had been executed by the Sheriff's Department alone - who knows).

Much to the disappointment of the law enforcement agencies involved there was no one on the commune except for one of the brahmins and a couple of the brahmacarinis. The brahmin had decided to stay to try to dismantle the puja arrangements properly or in the alternative perform a lesser version than had originally been intended, fearing the potential wrath of the decidedly wrathful goddesses whom had been promised their several pounds of flesh more than the imminent raid which we had been tipped off about. The brahmacarinis had stayed to support the brahmin and also out of a misplaced sense of duty, not willing to see the project die despite the fact that the writing on the wall indicated that we were all less than two minutes to midnight.

When the raid happened the brahmacaris who had executed the more dreadful sacrifices had already disappeared into the legally questionable slums of south Boston, courtesy of my aging Gremlin (and that was the last interstate trip she ever made, poor girl). The lone brahmin still on the Alabama property had, damnably enough in his indecision about the planned yajnas, kept a few of the goats tethered in a rusted-out shed near the ashrama trailer (three goats and a lawn-mower) instead of turning them loose or killing them and dumping the bodies (the latter which would have been the wisest decision) and so he ended up being charged. As it turned out his green card was fake so rather than going through a lengthy process in the local courts he ended up finding himself in a federal immigration facility (much higher security than the local jail, all things considered) for nine months before being shipped back to Kerala. The brahmacarinis ended up being underage and were not charged, instead being returned to the custody of their parents (said custody which they absconded almost immediately afterward, moving on to another town -

another mission project).

I stayed in Boston for a time afterward until other vistas called and though I have always stayed loyal to my spiritual master I never had a taste of ashrama life like I did back in Alabama. It has now been several years since I have seen RDG but an opportunity to do so arose not too long ago when I was back in Southie visiting family and as it turned out he was in town as well visiting some of my godbrothers and godsisters.

On a hot July afternoon, in that sort of steamy summertime atmosphere only possible in the cities, when the heat-waves coming off the pavement are visible and the kids play by the fire hydrants being bled of excess pressure, I reuinted with my spiritual master and some of my godbrothers and godsisters from back during the Alabama days. Although the heat was comparable, the atmosphere was not - a private garage and a tarmac blocked off from street view by large chain-link fences weaved through with black plastic security barriers in order to not give the local car-thieves too much of an eye-full.

The smell of smoke and meat wafted across the lot, done in a proper smoker this time and the smell as well as the sight of my eternal spiritual master, His Holiness Rudra das Goswami, brought me back to a time when my Krishna Consciousness was just burgeoning in the strangest of situations but oh, what interesting times they were. During this visit I had the opportunity to sit down for a lengthy discussion with RDG, part of which was recorded and

PURUSHAMEDHA

which has been transcribed here for the transcendental benefit of the readers. Many thanks to Rati-manjari for facilitating the recording and transcription.

PURUSHAMEDHA

FIRESIDE CHAT QUESTIONS:

(**KD** = Kumbhakarna dasa, **RDG** = Rudra das Goswami)

QUESTION 1.

KD: In Srimad-Bhagavatam 12th Canto we have descriptions of what the earth planet will become as the Iron Age progresses along the 427,000 years remaining of the Kali-yuga.

Though you know well the horrors described *Maharaja* - for the benefit of those receiving your siksa - I can name a few, namely, that by the end of the Kali-yuga human flesh will be sold on the open market; the sun will become large and malignant and scorch the earth so that trees will be the size of shrubs with roots and the flesh of others as the only sustenance; human bodies will become stunted, sexual activity will commence at an early age and people will be old by the time two decades have past; tyrants will rule from totalitarian outposts in the metropolitan areas forcing the vast majority of the population to take shelter underground, etc. In short, a real terrestrial hell.

Clearly, these pastimes for the individual living entities, parts and parcels of the Supreme Personality of Godhead, Lord Krsna, are meant for His ultimate pleasure. Yet some Vaisnavas under the auspices of invoking the Golden Age within the Kali-yuga due to the appearance of Lord Caitanya Mahaprabhu in this particular Kali-yuga (the appearance of this hidden avatara which comes only once

PURUSHAMEDHA

in a Day of Brahma) believe that the effects of the Kali-yuga can be beaten back - up to and including restoration of Vedic civilization, varna-asrama, etc. How should the devotees rectify this seeming contradiction?

RDG: This question is of great importance for two reasons. First, because it allows us to correct some bad understanding of shastra. Second, because it provides some understanding of Krsna's plan for the future.

The Vedas and Puranas are very clear that all time is cyclical, and that we move from one yuga to the next yuga. The Satya yuga (golden age) gives way to the Treta yuga (silver age), the Treta yuga (silver age) to the Dvapara yuga (bronze age), the Dvapara yuga (bronze age) to the Kali yuga (black age), then the cycle repeats. That is how Krsna designed the material universe, and there is literally no force or demigod or asura that can stop the wheel. It cannot be slowed, it cannot be resisted. Remember that we are on one small planet in a vast cosmos of worlds. As humans, our nescience blinds us and makes us self-centered. We think that we are the center of the universe, and that is what separates us from the Supreme Reality (Brahman Effulgence), and its source, the August Personage of KRSNA. Now as the yugas turn, Krsna descends again and again to save us from ourselves. He instructs us in the different methods to reach him. Now Krsna does not change, He is eternal, but culture changes, worlds change, nature changes, and the guna-quality of the cosmos changes too. Religion always – *always* – has the same goal: to reunite us with Krsna. But the form of religion changes. So in the

Satya Yuga, Krsna had very high standards, since the devas and rishis had very advanced spiritual knowledge. They had to do the highest level of religion practices to please Krsna, since even devas and rishis are technically separate from the August Personage. So the Vedas give very, very complex rites and mantras. In the Treta and Dvarpa yugas, the practices were a little less rigorous than in the Satya yuga, but they were still more rigorous than we are able to do today.

Now the Lord says clearly,

> *harer-nama harer-nama harer-namaiva kevalam kalau nasty-eva nasty-eva nasty-eva gatir anyatha*

Which means,

> 'The Mahamantra (harinam) is the only way to reach Krsna. In the Kali yuga, there is no other way!'

So we know that in the Kali Yuga, the basis of sadhana is *harinama*. A devotee must be practicing *Harinama*. Now that doesn't mean exclusively either – we do kirtan, we do yagnas, we offer prasada. But it means that the core of the sadhana is harinam. All Vaisnavas know this, there is no dispute about this fundamental practice. But in the earlier yugas – let's say the Satya yuga – then it was not this simple. Maharishi Daksha didn't just chant *harinama*, and if he had done this as the core of his sadhana, it would not have been enough, see? Because Krsna tells the devotees in each yuga what practice is the best practice for that yuga. We are living in a desperate age where most of the holiness has left, and so we have only the most basic, most primitive practices left to us. And because of this, some devotees think that the *harinama* is somehow better than the Vaisnava practices of the earlier yugas, and that is a fundamental error coming from nescience and arrogance.

Now, Krsna goes further than this. He makes it clear that many of the earlier practices have been compromised. He even descends at first as Lord Buddha, and later Lord Caitanya, to put a stop to some practices that had ceased to work. In Lord Buddha's time, most of the brahmana did not really know how to do sacrifices anymore. Oh sure, they knew how to slaughter an animal, but anyone can kill an animal. Sacrifice needs to be done correctly with the right understanding, right mantras, right yantras. So the Buddha, he sees that people are not sacrificing, they are just killing and eating the animals, and so he puts a moratorium on the practice. He doesn't say sacrifice is evil by nature, but that it is harmful to the Brahmins of his day, and so he prohibits it being performed except under very special circumstances. Buddha also completely changed sannyasa. Sannyasa is originally part of the āśrama or life-stages which came in the earliest yuga. When someone was elderly, they would not stay on in the home as a burden, but rather retire to the woods and concentrate on religion. Sometimes, a pious person would adopt it earlier. Back then you could do it, because the culture had formed around the idea that a sannyasi is special and should be given food and shelter whenever possible. So if you were a sannyasi, you didn't really have to beg, see? If you were

PURUSHAMEDHA

near a village, people would feed you, because someday the villagers would be sannyasi, and they'd want someone to feed them too! It was a smart system. But eventually, you had young people who were lazy and didn't want to work, and they'd take sannyasa and expect people to worship them. This is where you find people beginning to bow to sannyasis and worship them and fawn over them. Shameful, and it contradicts the entire idea of what the Vedas were trying to teach people. Sannyasa is about humility, not being spoiled like someone's pet! So by the time of Lord Buddha, many people were pretending to be sannyasis. Well, Lord Buddha didn't like this at all, so he reformed the asrama. People had to get rid of all their clothes, wear robes, and go door to door with a begging bowl, and they had to share all the food. No keeping your own food, you really had to share. But then the orthodox Brahmins didn't like this new stage of dharma, so they called Buddha a trickster and drove the Dharma out of India. This is why Buddhism isn't in India, it was accepted in the eastern lands instead.

But Krsna doesn't give up. He loves us too much! So again, the Lord descends as Caitanya. And he repeats what he said as the Buddha:

asvamedham gavalambham
sannyasam palapaitrkam
devarena sutopattim
kalau panca vivarjayet

Which means,

PURUSHAMEDHA

'In the Kali yuga, five things are unlawful: horse-sacrifice, cow-sacrifice, renunciation (**sannyasa**), ancestor worship, and siring a child on the sister-in-law.' (Krsna-jnama Khanda 185.180).

Now, clearly, Lord Caitanya was speaking contextually. We need to see what he did when he said this. We know that he condemns sannyasa, but he still initiated people into the renounced order. So clearly, this needs careful thought. My guru, Sri Sankarsana Goswami, told me that all the great Vaisnava acaryas agreed that sannyasa is still valid. So we must accept that Lord Caitanya was not prohibiting the order of sannyasa entirely. Rather, he was doing what the Lord Buddha had done earlier – he was prohibiting people from pretending to take it on, because it leads so easily to corruption. Too many people today claim to be sannyasa, but they have houses, bank accounts, cars, women, and they're still claiming to be devotees. Lord Caitanya was trying to put a stop to it, so he means that in general, sannyasa is forbidden. But sometimes, if you have a genuine sannyasi, and he finds a genuine student, he can offer it exceptionally. And this is the argument that all the Gaudiya-Vaisnava use when they have to interpret this tricky verse.

Now, here's the rub: if a Vaisnava accepts this argument, then he has to read the entire verse. If you agree that exceptionally one can accept sannyasa, then you have to agree that exceptionally, animal sacrifices are still valid, and so is ancestor worship, and insemination for a widowed sister-in-law. You have to accept this, there's no choice. You can't pick and choose with sashtra, you either accept it or you don't. No double-dipping, as we say in the States [smile]!

So why did Lord Caitanya discourage animal sacrifices? Well actually, he didn't. He had no problems with it at all, just like he had no real problems with genuine sannyasa. But the Muslims who were ruling India made it illegal for anyone to slaughter animals – except for Muslims! This was an economic decision, you see, because abattoirs make a lot of money, and the Muslims couldn't eat meat from a non-Muslim butcher. So they outlawed the practice of animal slaughter, and consequently the Vaisnavas became vegetarian in protest. They didn't want to pay the Muslims for their *halal* beef, for which the Muslims were charging extraordinary sums of money if the buyer was Hindu. You see? And so Lord Caitanya had to deal with this context. So he doesn't say "sacrifice is wrong", but rather, "sacrifice has become impossible in the Kali yuga, just like sannyasa has become impossible."

Hinduism also used to be extremely sexual. Look at Krsna, I mean he is absolutely a playboy. He's literally screwing every girl in a pretty skirt. And that's fine in Hinduism, because *kama* (sexual pleasure) is commanded in the Vedas. But the Muslims didn't like naked statues or the kama sutra, so the Vaisnava became ultra-puritanical, even more pruding than the Muslims. Do you see? Muslims eat meat, so we're too holy to eat meat. Muslims restrict nudity, so we'll restrict sex. It's a bit silly, but it was a way of preserving dignity.

PURUSHAMEDHA

Of course, once the Muslims were overthrown and the Hindus were able to practice freely, sacrifices returned immediately, and vegetarianism almost disappeared except among certain puritanical Brahmin families. Now as you can guess, some modern Vaisnavas don't like to hear this, they say 'oh no, the Vaisnavas are pure devotees. No sex, no sacrifice, just chanting all day.' So then we need to look at the recent history of the Vaisnava. The British, you know, spent a lot of time in India. Say what you like about their government, their religious scholars did a lot of good. They documented and cataloged a lot of the practices of the Vaisnava from the 18th and 19th centuries. I've read a lot of the British records on the Vaisnavas, and you know what they say? They say that the Saivites were more proper! The Vaisnava were all acting like Krsna, so they were cross-dressing, drinking, and fucking like teenagers. Even the older people were not the respectable uncles and aunties of today. No, they were really wild! So we know that the Vaisnavas of today are not the Vaisnavas of 100 years ago or more. And sacrifice, blood sacrifice, ancestor worship, sex, they were all considered Vaisnava practices. So when people today say 'Vaisnava don't practice sacrifice, because Lord Caitanya outlawed it', they are wrong according to recent historical documents, and wrong according to sashtra, because they will then have to explain why sannyasa are permitted and other acts are prohibited.

So, to answer your original question: can we turn back the wheel? I answer you: did Buddha say the wheel can be turned back? No, he said that the Dharma had continued forward. Did Caitanya say differently? No, Caitanya also said that the Dharma had to change with time. We cannot push the wheel backwards. Now, you might ask, can we push the wheel forwards? That's a different question entirely. The Sri Kalki Purana paints a picture of the end times where the Dharma has disappeared, everyone is insane or demonic, and the only righteous Vaisnavas are the ones who are sacrificing animals and worshipping Vishnu and practicing the Vedas, just like the family of Sri Kalki will be. Let me say this again: Lord Kalki's family will be practicing horse sacrifice, cow sacrifice, purushamedha even. That is the kind of family in which Lord Kalki will choose to be born, in the Kali Yuga. And the culture will be entirely demonic until he cleans it up.

What then should we do now? We hasten the turning of the wheel, by creating the conditions in which Lord Kalki will choose to descend. We foster the tamasic (dark) culture that He will delight to fight against. We revive the Vedic rites and sacrifices, which will characterize his own immediate family. Everything that is in the Sri Kalki Purana, we work to bring it about, so as to facilitate the context into which He has promised us he will be born. The wheel cannot turn back, but it can be moved forward a little faster.

QUESTION 2.

KD: The last several decades at least (beginning strongly in the nineteen-nineties) have seen many North American Vaisnavas take shelter of Gaudiya Matha spiritual masters in the Gaudiya Matha proper, from mathas based in India, outside of the auspices of the International Society for

Krishna Consciousness which was the main face of Vaisnavism in North America since the late nineteen-sixties.

Even before that - ISKCON devotees (with a predominant sector from the high-tier leadership of that society making up the prime demographic) after the disappearance of HDG Srila Prabhupada were taking shelter of Gaudiya Matha spiritual masters (HDG Srila Prabhupda's godbrothers for the most part) in order to learn the more esoteric side of Gaudiya Vaisnava way - namely bhajana over sadhana, raganuga bhakti over sadhana bhakti and leading into the very intimate practices of siddha-pranali, etc.

What is the premium placed on realization of the siddha-deha (genuine spiritual identity either on Goloka Vrindavana or the Vaikuntha planets) via sundry occult methods in the teachings of your spiritual master, His Divine Grace Sankarsana Dasa Thakura? How important is it to realize one's own siddha-deha in this lifetime and did your spiritual master ever reveal his own siddha-deha form to you and other intimate disciples?

RDG: First, we need to understand what *siddha-deha* means as a spiritual concept. Siddha-deha is your real essence, the real you. It is not the composite character that you think of as yourself in this current body. If we understand that we have all taken rebirth countless times, then we must also understand that there must be an original birth or incarnation which was determined not by karma, but by Krsna's immutable will. So, what is this original form? Through meditation and prayer and sadhana, we can get some hints, but this is very tricky. Even non-Vaisnava can get glimpses of a former life, and often this is as much delusion as it is memory. If you speak to advocates of past lives, they often speak about having been famous rulers, or celebrities, or sometimes notorious figures. Very few people report past lives as farmers, or clerics, or beggars. In India, many people report past lives as a great sadhu or even as an aspara or devata. Wow (you say), what sins they must have committed to take rebirth in the mortal world, eh? Why is this? It's because the overwhelming majority of past life histories are just illusion. On your own, you can't tell what is a dream or what is real. So what do we do? We rely on the spiritual master. The spiritual master is uniquely empowered through advanced sadhanas and bhakti to help uncover your real being. This can take many years of devotional service, or it can be immediate.

Let me given an example from my own experience. When I entered the service of Sri Sankarsana das Goswami, I was very interested in past lives. My Catholic seminar hadn't in any way encouraged that kind of thinking and I wasn't Indian-born, so it was all very exciting to me. Secretly, I hoped that I'd been some kind of wild animal, like a tiger or a bear, because I always likes big fierce creatures, or a bandit hero like Robin Hood. But when I tried to get my master to tell me about my past lives, he'd always change the subject, or tell me to go do chores, or get me to read sashtra. So I learned to stop asking, and eventually I didn't even think much about it. After all, unless you know your siddha-deha for certain, speculation is really not practical. I wouldn't go so far as to call it useless, but it's really just an exercise in imagination unless someone can tell for you sure what your original essence is.

Then one night, we had some devotees bring my gurudev an offering of a very nice brandy. Now I've said many times that Sankarsana didn't mind alcohol, but he wasn't really fond of it. The one exception to this was brandy – he did like it, and so once in a while someone would bring him a small bottle of "the good stuff". Then after a good tumbler or two, he'd be in a right jolly mood, and sometimes this predisposed him to be less taciturn than normal. Well on this one evening, there was a terrific storm with a lot of thunder and rain, and so we were all huddled inside the small salon with our master. Sankarsana decided to open the bottle of brandy, and soon he became less dour and more mellow. In fact he seemed so relaxed that I thought he might doze off (this happened sometimes), and his eyes took on a heavy-lidded quality that one associates often with very large reptiles when they are sunning themselves on a hot day.

After one particular crack of thunder, my gurudev's eyes flickered open, and he pointed at me. Now up until this day, he had always called me by my Christian name, or else "son". But then he said, "Hey, Rudra das, fetch me the bottle, I will have some more brandy." My god-brother Sanatana das was holding the bottle, and so he passed it to me. I was a bit surprised, and thought maybe I had misheard my guru. But I poured the old man another tumbler full of the liquor. He took another sip and smiled. "Lord Rudra serves Sankarsana so faithfully, he is the best of the Vaisnava. You are not him, but you were an *asura* in his service, and so you serve Sankarsana by serving lord Rudra. This is why you have such great fortune, even for a demon. Jai Krsna, I almost envy you to be in Lord Rudra's service directly!" And later, he explained to me what was a marut (wind demon), and what qualities such a being would have, and then by extension what special sadhana I should be adopting to please Rudra, and thereby please Sri Tamasi, who is non-different from Krsna.

So the short answer is this: you need to know you siddha-deha, but you can't do it alone. You need to attach yourself to your guru and serve him with pure devotional service, and this is allows him to discover the truth of who you are. Once he knows this, he knows better how to teach you, and more importantly, what he is supposed to be teaching you.

QUESTION 3.

KD: In our discussion thus far you have really indicated a good deal about how what is "acceptable" within Vaisnavism has greatly mutated in the concourse of the time prior to Muslim invasion of India, during and post this period. Many Vaisnavas have often repeated the dictum that while Krsna is obviously the absolute and unquestioned Supreme Personality of Godhead that we should avoid following his example - in other words - we should not attempt to engage in transgressive activities.

What is your take on this - how do we disciples answer this kind of reasoning and what example should the bhaktas

PURUSHAMEDHA

and bhaktins be following in this regard for those devotees who want to immerse themselves in Krsna Consciousness "without limits"?

RDG: This is a very timely question. I think the answer has two parts: first, how did the Muslims affect India and the Dharma; second, who is our ultimate role model?

To answer the first part, it is known through multiple sources (Indian and Muslim) that the Muslim conquest was tremendously difficult for the different families within Hinduism. Prior to the Muslim conquest, there is almost no evidence of vegetarianism. The only books that promote vegetarianism come from after the Mughal period. In the pre-Islamic period, you have instead records of rajas and princes organizing very lavish sacrifices of cows and horses, even humans in the purushamedha. There was no stigma against it, and you see echoes of it in the Sri Kalki Purana, where Lord Kalki will usher in a new golden age through performance of the Asvamedha rite. So it cannot be sinful now but be obligatory later, that is frank stupidity.

So what happened? Well, when the damn Arabs and Persians invaded, they wanted to abolish Hinduism, but they lacked the resources to do it entirely. So instead, what they did is attack the economic structure that supported the temples and the larger economy. A key example: since the priests depended on the revenues for doing the animal sacrifices, the Muslims passed news that forbid the slaughter of any animals, unless it was done by a halal (Muslim) butcher. So while the Muslims weren't making

PURUSHAMEDHA

Hinduism illegal, they were directly attacking a central practice. The Brahmins only ate meat that came from sacrifices, and they were not about to support the Muslim butchers. And this also cut into the Brahmin's revenues and their ability to validate the Ksatriya rulers. If the brahmins could no longer do sacrifices of any kind, what use were they to the people? So they stopped receiving sponsorship from the state, which was a terrible blow to them as a caste.

Well, how did the Brahmins retaliate? Almost collectively, they announced that real Hindus were not meat eaters, they were vegetarians. Bingo! It was really an overnight thing. You don't need to take my word for it, just go to your library and consult a book written by Muslims or Hindus during the Mughal period – this is all well documented by all sides. Significantly, Lord Caitanya himself came from this period, and he was himself a big promoter of this "reform Hinduism". And on a similar note, you can see that in the

PURUSHAMEDHA

parts of India that Islam didn't really enter, this vegetarianism didn't take root the same way. Take the Tamil region – they were never under the boot of the Muslims as was the mainland, and so animal sacrifices continued appropriately, and so did meat eating.

Of course, the Brahmins needed to find sacred texts to justify this, and that was a major problem, because the Vedas call for animal sacrifice. So what to do? Well, at this point, some very clever Vaisnavas began to remember that there were some minor texts that were much later, like the *Bhagavad Gita* and *Srimad Bhagavatam*, which had suggestions of vegetarianism. I know that many Vaisnava claim that these texts are the be-all and end-all of Vaisnava theology, but there lies another problem. Prior to the Mughal period, there is very rare mention of them! Hinduism produced a lot of books and commentaries, but very few of them even mention the Gita or the Srimad Bhagavatam. If they were really the celebrated texts that they are made out to be today, then all the Vaisnava sects would have been mentioning them. But instead, everyone was quoting Vedas, interpreting Vedas, and practicing Vedas. The Vedas only fall into disuse when the Muslims are in power, and unfortunately even after the Muslims were driven out, many Vaisnava have refused to return to the Vedas. Instead, we see the Gita and Srimad and newer literatures called "Vedic Literatures", when they really have almost nothing to do with the Vedas.

When you tell other Vaisnava this, they get really angry. Well don't let them get mad – just ask them to produce any

Hindu text prior to the Mughal period which mentions Krsna. There are hardly any, did you know? Before the Mughal period, he is always Lord Visnu. That is why we are called *Vaisnavas*, not *Krsnavas*. But since Krsna presented a form of Hinduism that did not threaten the Muslims (and how could he, the little rascal?), that is the form of God that we continue to embrace as the supreme Lord.

To answer the second part of your question, well it is a good one. You said: how should we act? I answer: whom do you worship? We worship Krsna. Well, Sankarsana das always used to say that Krsna is a little sociopath. He is a little monster. He sets up all the rules, just like dominos, and then he proceeds to knock them all down! Even in the Mahabharata, he is always helping the Pandavas to cheat in warfare. Krsna understands that in broad terms, society needs some rules. That is why He gives us the Vedas, and the Vedas give us some rules. But once society is set up and the rules are being carried out, then Krsna causes all kinds of mischief. This is not because He is mean or cruel without reason, but because He doesn't want us to worship the rules, He wants us to worship him.

Take Krsna and Radha. Now, every culture takes marriage very seriously. Adultery is a major crime, right? But Krsna commits adultery with Radha, wow! That is a terrible sin. But He does it – and this is important – the sashtra tells us about it. Krsna wants you to know that he fucked a married woman. Why is this? It is so that you see that the rules are guidelines that are supposed to lead you to Him. Sometimes, though, the rules don't work the way they are supposed to work. When that happens, the Vaisnava should follow Krsna's example. Radha was really Laksmi, She was ultimately married to Krsna, and so Krsna was not really sinning – but our bad human reasoning made it look that way.

Let me say this differently: Sankarsana das used to say that our only real priority in life is to worship Krsna, to love Krsna, to be like Krsna. Krsna followed the rules and codes until those rules and codes separated Him from His beloved. Then He broke the rules without a second thought. So how can you and I act any differently?

Now some swamis would say that we should follow Lord Caitanya. Well, I agree entirely, because Lord Caitanya was a rule breaker too. He refused to do sacrifices, even though it was a rule to do *yajnas*. Instead, he taught people to do *harinama*, which no one had ever heard of before. So people broke the rules and started to do *harinama*. The Muslims wanted the Hindus to rebel so that they would have an excuse to kill them, but Caitanya was too smart, he played along. Caitanya told people to be honest, but he was a liar himself: when people asked him to acknowledge his divinity, he refused categorically. You see, he was a trickster, because the rules had stopped working. And the day will come when He will return as Lord Kalki, and then the game will change. Then it will be His turn to slaughter the Muslims, don't you doubt it! Then it will be time to bring back the rules, and then He will expect people to follow them again. Kalki is a law-restorer, but the Buddha was not, and Caitanya was not. They were tricksters, like

PURUSHAMEDHA

Krsna himself.

So how should we act? We need to be tricksters, rebels, spiritual ruffians. We follow the social rules and taboos, until the moment that they restrain us from Krsna. When that moment comes, and the rules become a barrier between you and God, then *fuck* the rules. They don't matter. We are not Christians or Muslims – we don't believe in some awful law or day of judgment. We know that God is all that matters, and that He himself breaks His laws to set an example.

Remember:

>Through Krsna, we become truly liberated.

>>Only through Krsna,

>>>Can we become truly liberated.

PURUSHAMEDHA

SATTVA, RAJAS, TAMAS

When I stayed with Sri Sankarsana das Goswami at first, I didn't know exactly what I was supposed to do. Where many ashrams and temples today seem to have a certain natural rhythm that all the devotees follow, my spiritual master's home was always a little bit chaotic. Not chaotic in the sense that there was any particular wildness or disorganization, but chaotic in that everyone was really doing their own thing. When I was doing chores, my godbrothers and godsisters were sometimes outside chanting, or singing, or reading shastra. If I was reading shastra, someone else was being tutored by Sankarsana. There wasn't a lot of privacy and the walls were thin, so sometimes this lead to some mild embarrassment. I remember one afternoon, for example, when my master was trying to explain raganuga bhakti to me, and I was having a hell of a time understanding how true devotion could be so utterly lawless. Sankarsana was incredibly patient, but in the middle of him reciting some passage from the Bhagavad Gita, I became aware of a gentle, steady thudding from the room above the salon. At first I thought that someone was doing some cleaning, but that was quickly corrected I heard one of the female devotees crying out each time the floor thudded. Sankarsana das pretended not to hear it and tried to continue lecturing from the shastra, but then the banging upstairs became louder and louder. My spiritual master grimaced, but then he began to chuckle in a rueful, good natured way, and waved a gnarled hand towards the ceiling. "See?" he said, "I am trying to explain raganuga bhakti, but Priya devi dasi is actually demonstrating it with

Balarama das right now." I was shocked, honestly, that he wasn't upset. The situation was a bit embarrassing, as the house wasn't very large, and I asked my master if maybe we should continue the lesson later. He shook his head, but stood up and motioned me out the door and into the small kitchen that was adjacent to the small salon that doubled as our classroom.

Sankarsana das Goswami opened one of the small cupboards in the dingy little kitchen, and began to rummage for something. Eventually he found what he was looking for, and brought out a small tray with three small tubs of paste. One was white, one was red, and one black. They appeared to be some kind of coarse glue or paint, through the consistency seemed as if tending towards a very thick paste. He looked at me for a moment and frowned pensively.

"Balarama and Priya – it's my fault that they're screwing around," and he pointed vaguely at the ceiling. "You know that they wouldn't normally do it during the day. But their rajas right now is very intense, and so they are both suffering from a great deal of passionate devotion."

I didn't know what he meant by rajas, so I had to ask for clarification.

"Son, it's like this," he said. "Krsna creates Lord Visnu, and Lord Visnu creates all the material universe. Each universe has three main material elements. In Sanskrit we call them the three *Gunas*, and they are *Sattva, Rajas, Tamas*. Light,

PURUSHAMEDHA

Passion, and Darkness. Everything you see and hear and touch – they are at some level a mix of these three things. Even people have these, but everyone has a different mix. So do animals. A tiger is very violent, and so she has a great deal of *rajas* (passion). A monkey has a lot of cleverness, so he has a great deal of *sattva* (light). And the turtle has great endurance and longevity, which comes from *tamas* (darkness).

Is one better than the other, I asked.

"Oh no," he said, frowning, "you need to have all three of them. Lord Visnu doesn't make mistakes. But sometimes your equilibrium changes naturally, or if you have a good guru, he can adjust it for you, so that you experience the world differently. Right now, Priya and Balarama are experiencing a serious surge in rajas, and so they're fucking like animals whenever they're not fighting. And when they're not fucking or fighting, they're chanting and worshiping with great intensity. But they need to experience it, because it is part of them developing spontaneous love of Krsna. They need to either push past the heat to get to Krsna, or else use the heat for Krsna. It's all the same in the end, because it's all Krsna. But they'll go through it, and they'll know Krsna more intimately than they did before." And he smiled in a sly way that seemed somewhat inappropriate for a guru, but I came to understand later that he was really no prude, and didn't suffer prudes in his company.

And here, he turned his gaze back to the three jars of paste. He seemed to decide on the white paste, and taking the jar in his calloused hand, he told me close my eyes. I did so, and I felt him beginning to apply the paste as if it were tilaka. When I opened my eyes, he was beaming at me.

"Jai Krsna," he mused, "you're in for quite a week." And then he told me to go about my chores for the day, as my lesson was done.

So I did my chores, and then ate some supper with the other devotees. Priya and Balarama joined us midway through supper, and they didn't seem at all embarrassed for the noise, nor did anyone give them a hard time (pardon the pun!). Then after dinner, I thought perhaps that I would review the shastra that Sankarsana das had been trying to explain to me. I headed back into the house, and picked up the battered copy of the *Gita* which my master had been using for my sake. Of course he had it memorized, but he wanted the devotees to read it for themselves. Finding a space on the tired low couch, I began to read the Gita.

Jai Krsna, I thought to myself, it's really an amazing book. So much in here, and I couldn't see ANY of this before. What a great teacher my guru is, eh? As I read line after line, layers and layers of meaning began to appear to me that I'd never even noticed were there. What had initially appeared a one-layered conversation between Arjuna and Krsna suddenly transformed into an intricate and intensely meaningful discussion that had five or ten different subtexts and layers that no one had ever explained to me before.

Hours flew by, and so did the night. The next thing I knew, it was morning. I was still reading when I realized that Sankarsana das was sliding a small tin mug of coffee onto a small table nearby.

"Hey, fella", he smiled indulgently, "enough reading for now. Drink some coffee, then it's time for your lesson."

I drank the coffee in great excited gulps, and somehow managed not to burn myself in the process. When Sankarsana das sat down across from me on his chair, I had every intention of paying close attention (as I normally would). But when my master began to lecture, I thought my head would explode. While previously I had understood that my master had great wisdom, now when he spoke, it was as if I was hearing Krsna Himself speaking. Where before I had heard the Gita expounded, it was like now hearing the Gita come alive and telling me the very secret of secrets.

Amazingly, I found myself to be a worthy pupil. It was as if somehow my guru had empowered me to be able to learn from his incredibly advanced teachings. Not only did I understand what he was saying, but I asked questions that pleased him, and showed that I was able to understand not only the explicit meanings but also the implicit secrets from Krsna's instructions in the chariot. I was doing pretty well to keep up with the older man, and I began to feel a certain sense of satisfaction with my newly attained learning.

Immediately, midway through one sentence, as I felt a particular surge of pride, Sankarsana suddenly stabbed me in the forehead with one calloused finger.

"There!" he growled, "right there! Kill your pride, fella! You are a good boy, but you're not Arjuna. Jai Krsna, I'm nowhere near Arjuna. You're doing well, but you're not getting even a tenth of what Arjuna was getting from Krsna, not even a tenth of a tenth. But what you are getting (and here he leaned close) is a good dose of Krsna, seen through the window of sattva. You'll feel this for a few more days, and then you'll begin to drift back towards your usual equilibrium. But enjoy it while it lasts."

Well, I did. For another two or three days, I read voraciously. My godbrothers and godsisters left me alone, and didn't even trouble me with chores. People brought me food, and I ate sparingly, just enough to keep reading. There weren't enough books or lessons, I just devoured knowledge. But eventually the sattva began to lessen in me, and my reading slowed. Other things began to assert themselves, like my need for company, or food, or sleep(!).

A few days later, Sankarsana das called me back into the house, and lead me back to the kitchen. Again he pulled out his little tray of jars, and this time he applied the red paste to my forehead. It smelled faintly like tiger balm, and it burned a little when he had applied it. Then we did my usual lesson, but this time I felt no particular mental sensation. In fact, if anything, I felt restless and impatient, and sensing this in me, my master excused me early and sent me out.

Jai Krsna, I remember thinking, what a great place this is. Such good people, such nice godbrothers and godsisters. I should really be doing more to help. They all take such good care of me, and so does Krsna. Oh, I love Krsna. Oh, I love Krsna and Radha so much. What a candala I am, but I'll show them – I'll be the best devotee ever.

That week, I could hardly read at all. Where previously I had felt practically brahminical in my mental powers, now I felt like a man on fire for Krsna and Radha. I was so fired up for Krsna that I could hardly sleep. And when I did sleep, wow! The dreams! I'd be transported to Vrindavan, and together with Krsna, I'd find myself sporting with the gopis in the forest. While Krsna was ardently embracing Radha, I found myself entwined with Revati (who sounded suspiciously like Priya devi dasi). Anyway, hot dreams lead to inflamed days, and I channeled my passion into sweeping for Krsna, cleaning for Krsna, carrying wood for Krsna. I chanted 64 rounds a day, and would have chanted more if Sankarsana das hadn't forced me to continue lessons, which I'm ashamed to admit I had a hard time to sit through.

Eventually, maybe after a week or two, my head cooled, and I began to feel more "myself". And so again, as you can probably guess, Sankarsana das brought me back to the kitchen and brought out the three pastes. Soon my brow was smeared with the black tilaka, and it felt strangely cool and soothing.

"Son, do you know why we started with sattva?" he asked me curiously.

Of course, I did not, and admitted as much.

He pointed at the white jar. "Sattva comes first. It's the brahamcari's color. Light! Intelligence. Learning. Sattva dispels ignorance, helps us to understand. So a real devotee begins with sattva, but it's just the first step."

He pointed at the red jar.

"Rajas is passion. The householder needs it, the ksatriya needs it too. Kama sutra, eh. Rajas is ambition and desire and energy. People who do things have rajas, do you see? People who get things done, they are rajasic. Some people have no rajas – no fire, no passion. That's sad. Krsna has no use for a person without rajas. To really love Krsna, you NEED rajas. To understand how Krsna loves you? You really need rajas too."

Finally, the black jar. Here, he frowned as if concerned.

"Now some people, some fake gurus, they tell you that tamas is ignorance. How stupid! It's Sanskrit for darkness. Now this isn't the bad darkness of ignorance – it's the true darkness, the darkness of Sri Rudra, or Sri Sankarsana. The Srimad Bagavatam says that Lord Ananta is the very essence of tamas, so it can't be ignorance – even to suggest it or joke about it is a terrible offence. No, darkness is primordial. It is eternal, it is true abiding. To love Krsna with sattva is to love Krsna with your mind. To love Krsna with rajas is to love him passionately. But to love Krsna with tamas is the most dangerous kind of love, because it's innate love. Love that is deep, deep in your marrow. It's deeper than your mind. It's stronger and colder than rajas. It's the love that exists when all your mind and emotions have dried up and blown away. Do you see?"

Of course I didn't, and I knew not to lie. But he just laughed and affectionately slapped me on the shoulder. He told me it was alright, and that in time I'd understand.

He gestured for me to head outside, and I began to go. But when I was right at the front door to the house, my brain suddenly began to feel heavy. Tired, I said. Hadn't slept enough recently, so I ought to go lie down. So instead of heading to do my chores, I went to find a quiet tree to stretch out underneath, and to rest my eyes for a few minutes.

But I couldn't sleep. Even as I relaxed, a delicious new sensation began to creep over me. Krsna, I thought, of course, it's Krsna. A chill began to seep into my bones, and my mind began to slow down. I couldn't really think – if I could have, I would have worried that I was getting sick. But my brain felt mired, like an elephant that has slipped into deep mud and is sinking further down into the dark.

PURUSHAMEDHA

I was in a trance, or more accurately, I was almost in a coma. It's not that I was unconscious, but the entire world around me became muted and grey. Sounds were off, and colors were dulled. I felt like I was drifting deep underwater, and the only sensation that I could latch onto was a deep, terrifyingly real sense of Krsna's presence. This wasn't the bright, quick sensation of encountering Krsna in the Vedas, and it wasn't the fever dreams of Krsna and Radha. This was really terrifying. I experienced the complete loss of sensation from my body, and even my ego was briefly sublimated. All I could think of was the sense of an immense force, an intellect, that was both cruel and loving and malevolent, which was surrounding me and inside me and crushing me to paste. Krsna, a voice whispered inside me, it's all Krsna. Krsna, Krsna, Krsna. Krsna, I muttered dully, as if drugged, yes, of course, Krsna. Only Krsna.

If you ask me how long I was there, swooning, I honestly don't know. It might have been a few hours, but I think it was honestly a few days. When I finally came to, I was still under the tree. Someone had put a blanket over me, and I felt incredibly stiff, as if I had slept on hard ground. Where previously my face was clean shaven, now I felt hard bristle along my jaw. Dear God, I thought, what is my master doing to me.

Of course, this was something that Sankarsana put everyone through, not merely once, but repeatedly. And this was the reason largely for the chaos that was so characteristic of his home. Everyone who came into contact with him could not help but be changed, transformed, by

PURUSHAMEDHA

the powerful states of Krsna Consciousness that he provoked. And this was just one of the many amazing and fantastic (if not horrifying and terrific) gifts that he gave to his devotees, and for which I remain eternally grateful.

***

Love, without sattva, cannot be wise.
Love, without rajas, cannot be strong.
Love, without tamas, cannot be realized.

PURUSHAMEDHA

PURUSHAMEDHA
ON RAGANUGA BHAKTI

When I first arrived at the little ashram of Sri Sankarsana das Thakur, the first thing I noticed was that the few students who my master attracted were not all following the same spiritual practices. I don't mean there was nothing in common – there was a certain routine and rhythm to each day. The day began and ended around the same time, and meals were always around the same time. There were certain chores that everyone had to do, and my godbrothers and godsisters helped me find my place. There was a definite "pecking order", make no mistake! And there were some nasty practical jokes that a few of my godbrothers tried to pull, but the grace of my spiritual master protected me from any real harm, though I did get made to look like a fool once or twice.

But what I mean to say is that unlike some other ashrams I'd visited, you didn't find everyone chanting or singing together as a group very often. In fact, the ashram didn't have much sankirtan at all, it was very rare to see it. If I had to describe the ashram, it could be characterized by a certain stillness, a certain dreamy quietude that muffled sound. You would hear the droning of insects in the forest nearby and the sounds of quiet voices, but there was a certain heaviness to the place. When Sankarsana das was present, it was especially potent. It was like the sun just refused to shine there, except with a dull sullen glare on the brightest days. Sankarsana das liked the quiet, and there was a certain calm to the place that was not bad for meditation – as long as you stayed awake. Such was the power of my master, and I don't even think he did it consciously – but his essence or guna was so heavily tamasic that it literally soaked into the stones, wood, and bones of the place.

We all chanted. No question there, and it was not always 16 rounds a day – sometimes it was 10 or 12. But where others might have chanted more, Sankarsana das was more concerned about the potency of the chanting. "Jai Krsna!" he'd swear, "any candala can chant 34 rounds out of duty. That's not love, that's not devotional sevice. Krsna wants you to love him, not patronize him. If you love Krsna, you go slowly. You take your time. You savor the *harinama* – you roll it around your tongue, you taste each syllable. The mantra is Krsna, so show some damned respect, eh? "

Some days, I think he only chanted five or six rounds. But he chanted it so slowly, so intensely, that he'd be sweating from the effort. His eyes would become bloodshot and roll around like a drug addict, and his pronunciation was so slow that he'd sound like a dying man. His breathing would become haggard, and he would become faint. But you could really feel the devotion, and it wasn't just the regular "devotional mellow" that you see some would-be saints claim to feel. There was nothing mellow about this – it had all the levity of a man in the middle of a stroke. And when he'd be deep, deep in his devotional practices, sometimes some very strange things would happen around the ashram. We'd hear strange noises coming from around the house, especially from any of the sinks or drains. Animals would alternately swarm the house, or refuse to come anywhere within sight. It made for some very odd days and nights, to say the least! But it also drove home the point that this man was not like other gurus, in that his miracles were the result of genuine bhakti and not an attempt to show off for a crowd.

I expected Sankarsana das to give me some kind of regulative principles, because two of my godbrothers seemed to be following some kind of ascetic code. They chanted almost fifty rounds a day. They refused to eat meat, drink alcohol, or look at the female devotees, who take great pains to mock their godbrothers at every opportunity. In fact, thinking at first that this was Sankarsana's way, I began to emulate them. I started to ignore the girls, and one of them seemed genuinely hurt by my sudden piety. But my guru called me into his little salon one evening and told me to sit down. He poured me a little tea and poured some for himself too. He sat down across from me.

"Son", he said, "why are you starting to act like Ravi and Sukadev?"

I responded that since they were senior devotees, I thought I needed to follow their advanced example. Sankarsana laughed loud, then waved a heavy hand dismissively.

"Oh, they're not advanced at all!" he chuckled. "In fact they're in worse shape than you. They fell in with one of those foreign mission groups, and now all they want to do is chant Hare Krsna and ignore the girls. So sad! They don't know Krsna or the Rasa Lila dance at all, I guess. If I were younger, I would dance the Rasa Lila, but what is their excuse, I don't know at all." He frowned disapprovingly.

I didn't understand, and so I asked him about the regulative principles. Didn't we need to follow a series of codes and guidelines to help us love Krsna better?

"Listen," he said patiently, "have you read the Gita?"

I affirmed that I had.

"Good", he said, "and Srimad Bagvatam?"

Yes, I'd read that one too, several times.

"Well then," he paused, "do you see any regulation there? Is there anything about not looking or talking to girls, or staying at home and chanting all day?"

No, I confessed, I'd looked for those passages without finding them.

Krsna, Krsna, Krsna, he mused, why did you send me this boy? He is such a demon, but I will help him.

He turned back to me.

"Lord Krsna says in the Gita:

Even if one commits the most abominable actions, if he is engaged in devotional service, he is to be considered saintly

PURUSHAMEDHA

because he is properly situated. He quickly becomes righteous and attains lasting peace. O son of Kunti, declare it boldly that My devotee never perishes (9:30-31).

He paused, then recited:

How much greater then are the brahmanas, the righteous, the devotees and saintly kings who in this temporary miserable world engage in loving service unto Me. Engage your mind always in thinking of Me, offer obeisances and worship Me. Being completely absorbed in Me, surely you will come to Me (9:33-34).

He swallowed, and I could see his eyes beginning to take on that strange, bloodshot look he would get during chanting. He continued:

Always think of Me and become My devotee. Worship Me and offer your homage unto Me. Thus you will come to Me without fail. I promise you this because you are My very dear friend. Abandon all varieties of religion and just surrender unto Me. I shall deliver you from all sinful reaction. Do not fear (18:65-66).

He smiled gently then.

"So this is the secret knowledge of the Gita, the ultimate secret. So precious, it's not even in the Vedas. LOVE Krsna. Serve him, by any means, any means at all. If we are speaking of true love, limitless love, then there cannot be limits, eh? If you really say to someone "I would do anything for you", then you had better mean it."

PURUSHAMEDHA

I asked why Caitanya had instituted so many rules that sure LOOKED like regulation. He frowned and shook a finger at me.

"What kind of school did you skip, eh? Americans, no history except Pearl Harbor and the Nazis. Bah, no good at all. Look, when did Lord Caitanya appear?"

Of course, I safely answered it was in the medieval period. My teacher smirked openly.

"Oh, so you don't know, of course. It's not your fault, you just weren't taught well. I blame your teachers, ha. Lord Caitanya appeared in the 16th century. Do you know who controlled India during the 16th century?"

Of course I did: the Hindus, obviously!

He didn't like that answer at all, and he threw his teacup at me. I dodged and it shattered against the wall.

"*Jai Krsna!*" he cried, "it was the candala Muslims! Dogs and dog-fuckers all. They killed the brahmanas and smashed the temples, and they put out all the sacred fires. The stopped the *yajnas*, and when the *yajnas* stopped, the devas all left. No more sacred rites. No more offerings. No more ashmavedha, and with no ashmavedha, no more kings. No more purushamedha, so no more cosmic order. Kali Yuga gets worse and worse. The sign of the Kali Yuga is the abandonment of the Kali Yajna, ha."

PURUSHAMEDHA

I protested that I didn't know, and he growled but relaxed a little.

"Look, my boy, it's not your fault, but it's what the American sannyasis forget. Lord Caitanya appeared to help the Dharma survive. No more brahmana, no more sannyasa, nor more yajna, and the candala Muslims were killing anyone who fought back. This is known, it's in all the books. So what does Krsna do? He comes to help protect the dharma. He gives us the Hare Krsna yajna so that we have SOME little yajna. He tells people that sannyasa is really gone, since it became impossible to really renounce the city. Look at sannyasas today – are they in the forest, in caves? No, they're in the cities, driving cars or being driven like *Maharaj*a. That is not sannyasa. Anyway, Caitanya was not improving the Dharma. He was giving people a temporary form to use until the Muslims left."

He frowned.

"And they DID leave. Then we got back our temples. We got back our fires and our knives and our murtis. We were able to do yajna again, and most Vaisnava go back to the old ways. They follow the Vedas. We have cow sacrifice, horse sacrifice, man sacrifice. India becomes strong, the devas return. But some few Vaisnava, they don't want things to get better. Maybe they loved the Muslims or they want to be Muslim. So they continue to chant Hare Krsna, Hare Krsna, but they won't read Vedas! Won't do *yajnas*! So we look at them today, and they're all asuras and dog-fuckers, just like the Muslims. They're cheating whores, not devotees."

This was pretty strong language to hear, especially since he was referring to other Vaisnava. I tried to protest, but he wouldn't listen.

"Son, look. *Raganuga bhakti*. What does it mean? Crazy love. Crazy, teenager love. Layla-i-Qays love. Romeo and Juliet love. Love with no rules. No limits. No safe words, no games. Really wild, crazy, dangerous love. Look at Krsna and Radha – she's married, but he doesn't care. She doesn't care. They sneak into the woods, and he fucks her. Every chance she gets, she gets him alone and she takes off her clothes for him. Naughty girl, eh? Just like those American girls outside doing service. They want to take off their clothes for Krsna too, but they're not ready for that yet, and so He is making them wait."

This kind of talk made me frankly uncomfortable. But he didn't stop. He kept going.

"Don't blush, boy! This is raganuga bhakti. This is love. Love of Krsna. So how do we show Krsna that we love Him? Any way we can. You see, with Krsna, there is no sin. No sin. You understand? Look, when a man loves a girl, a pretty girl, he wants to impress her. So what does he do? Crazy things! Anything to get her attention. That's what Krsna wants from you. He wants you to go a little crazy for Him. Go get drunk for Krsna. Go steal something for

Krsna. Show Krsna that you will do anything, anything for him."

I replied that petty crime didn't seem like decent devotion to the Supreme Being. But Sankarsana just smiled knowingly. "Son, you say that now. But you don't really have limits, you know. You know why I took you in? Because you love Krsna. You don't know it yet, but Krsna is very deep in your heart. If not, you would not have found me. But you are an asura. You're a demon, an evil spirit in a man's body. So for you, Krsna doesn't want you to pick flowers for Him. Krsna doesn't just want you to chant and sing. No, Krsna made you a demon, so you need to love him like a demon."

Very reasonably, I had no idea what that even meant, so I asked him to clarify. He looked away.

"Oh, you'll know soon enough. I can't tell you, you need to be spontaneous. Because that's the other part of raganuga bhakti – no one can tell you how to do it. Your heart will know what kind of devotion Krsna wants. When you're out there in the world, you listen to your heart. Because Krsna made you what you are for a reason, so you need to learn to love Him in the way that He built you to. I can help you get started – I can show you how to listen, but only you can hear the voice."

And he did show me how to listen. Certain mantras helped. Fasting ekadasi is an important part. Prayers to my guru and his guru (Sri Lalita Prasad) opened the doors to levels of mercy that I could never have unlocked on my own. And eventually, bhakti began to well up from my heart like water from a stone. Unbidden and unlooked for, I began to intuit and to know what Krsna wanted. It was not a quick process, but it was quicker than I would have gone if I had followed the slower, drying path of regulation. Many have followed regulation for years, and died without ever tasting the sweetness of real, genuine love of Krsna.

With Sankarsana das Thakur's help, most importantly, I discovered what true holiness is. True holiness is not dryly following rules that run contrary to nature. It's not denying the flesh to please some sadistic god. Krsna is sadistic, but he's not into denying you pleasure – He hurts you by giving you want what you really want. Eventually, you realize that the things you want are all empty and tasteless, unless you're enjoying them for His sake. True holiness, rather, is living each day with an intimate, loving connection to Krsna. I've woken up some mornings in the street, still hazy from sleeping on concrete and starving. That is the price of serving a crazy god – you go a little crazy, and you are guided to do crazy things. I've broken my knuckles several times getting into drunken fights, where I pummeled someone who mocked Krsna. I defend Him as if I was defending my beloved. Because He is my beloved, and I'd knock out anyone's teeth for insulting Him. Once someone said to me that Prabhupada is equal is Krsna, and that fraud ended up picking several of his teeth off the ground. I spent the night in jail. But it was worth it, and the sheer joy of Krsna's pleasure is what keeps me going.

PURUSHAMEDHA

My hope for you, reading this, is that you find that same, spontaneous love of Krsna. That love without limits. It is crazy, and He is crazy, and you will not stay sane in loving Him. But you will find Krsna – you will genuinely see Him and touch Him, and that is worth any price. That is beyond any price.

हरे कृष्ण हरे कृष्ण
कृष्ण कृष्ण हरे हरे
हरे राम हरे राम
राम राम हरे हरे

PURUSHAMEDHA

DISAPPEARANCE OF HIS HOLINESS SRI SANKARSANA DAS GOSWAMI

On 10 November 2013, we endured the disappearance of His Holiness Sri Sankarsana das Goswami. The great acarya had battled cancer for several years and was very sick for several months, but continued an exemplary life of devotion to Radha-Krsna and Balarama up to his final hours.

Sri Sankarsana das Thakur was born in 1925 in Bengal. A distant cousin of Sri Bhaktivinoda Thakur, as a youth Sri Sankarsana attached himself to the service of Sri Lalita das and received initiation from him. With Sri Lalita das Thakur, he studied the Vedas and Puranas, and was a known expert in the all traditional brahminical sciences, especially in Raganuga Bhakti.

Sri Sankarsana das was known for his quick wit and biting tongue. He was unusual in that he gathered only a small group of disciples, as he believed in genuine austerity and extremes in devotional practices. He was the greatest living Vaisnava I ever had the privilege to meet. He was loved by some, envied by several, and known closely by only a few. He was a recluse – a sannyasi in the genuine sense of one who withdraws from society – but a kind-hearted fellow who deeply cared about the current state of Vaisnavism, and the Gaudiya branch in particular.

PURUSHAMEDHA

Before he was born, his parents received visions of Lord Ananta Nagaraja, the serpentine expansion of Krsna. Lord Ananta informed the parents that the child would be a great Vaisnava devotee, and that in a previous life he had been a prominent saint as well. Throughout his childhood and adult life, Sri Sankarsana was greatly attached to Lord Ananta, which marked him apart from many other Vaisnavas. He manifested various *siddhis* early in life, and was a master vamamarga adept at the time of his disappearance. He made pilgrimages throughout India to all the sites associated with Lord Balarama, who is understood to be the incarnation of Lord Ananta.

Sri Sankarsana das gathered few disciples and gave the vows of sannyasa to even fewer. He lived a life of true austerity, and expected the same from other sannyasis. He genuinely believed in humble living, and lived largely on rice, bread and water. People who visited his ashram likewise endured very humble accommodations. He was not a man concerned with what other people thought, and he kept to himself. In this regard, he was much like his acarya, Sri Lalita Thakur.

He had zero patience for the foreign sannyasis, who expect to be hosted and feasted like royalty in Vrindavan, always trying to teach Indians to "be Hindu". One of his favorite sayings to these fraudulent sannyasis was: *"Hare Krsna! So you're not Indian, you travelled first-class to get here, you're staying in a five star hotel, and you're eating three or four huge meals like a prince each day? Let me guess –* **Prabhupada sent you!**"

PURUSHAMEDHA

Yet Sri Sankarsana himself was no conservative prude, and did not suffer these neo-Hindus to preach their modern gospel of abstinence. His sexual appetite was healthy, and many married men in his region were genuinely jealous of his charisma. He is known to have had liaisons with several of his more attractive female devotees, of which he made no secret. He had the easy grace of a man with nothing to prove, and the confidence of one who had mastered very advanced siddhis through his austere practices.

Like His Holiness Sri Bhaktivinoda Thakur and His Holiness Sri Lalita das Thakur, Sri Sankarsana enjoyed a good meal of roasted meat or fish, and enjoyed consuming coffee and cigars when they were available. His few householder devotees would at times offer such gifts when they travelled to visit him. He drank alcohol occasionally, but did not care for it overmuch. But Sri Sankarsana das limited his intake of these things in keeping with the economic regulations of sannyasa. Strict moderation through limited frequency, he taught, was the key.

Sri Sankarsana taught us to not play favorites with the gunas. He would say: "Look, Vyasadeva taught us clearly in the Srimad Bhagavatam that Lord Ananta is Sri Tamasi – the Lord of Darkness (*tamas*). If Lord Ananta is the first expansion of Krsna and the source of Bhagavan Siva, then how can we shun *tamas*? It is to be treasured, but in its purer forms."

Sri Sankarsana das was a strict adherent of the Vedas. He took great pleasure in offering sacrifice to Sri Vishnu and the demigods, in accordance with the brahminical varna. He celebrated the *Asvamedha*, the gomedha, and he preached the purushamedha with great relish.

PURUSHAMEDHA

"Ah, sacrifice!" he would exclaim, "the Vedas ordain it, the Puranas commend it, and Sri Kalki will chop the heads off kings who don't do it!"

Several times, he also said: "The sign of the Kali Yuga is the abandonment of Kāli Yajna!"

Other gurus would tell students that it took years to learn even basic *siddhis*, but Sri Sankarsana said this was evidence of fraud. Right up until his death in November 2013, he taught his small group of disciples to put his knowledge to the test. "Look," he said, "don't accept my *jnana* at face value. Try these things out. If you get results, stay with me. If you don't get results, then I release you from your service to me – go and study with a teacher you can learn from." And he meant it, but he never lost a single student, and his disciples all went on to become potent adepts in their own right.

He was not showy and he did not care for material things, but he did not judge householders for wanting to enjoy the material, and he always reminded us that Sri Krsna and Sri Balarama enjoyed sports, food, dancing, music, and conjugal activities. So when people needed these things, and asked him for help, he would put forth his power and attract these things to those who needed them.

He did not like to do miracles, but I remember one particular night when a householder wife came very late, crying that her infant son was very ill. Without a word, he put on his coat and went with her. A few of us went with him to help. By the time we reached the house, the doctor was already there ahead of us – but it was no use, the boy was quite dead. The mother was understandably beside herself with grief, and cried so piteously that we were all worried that she would harm herself. We all begged the acarya to help, but he was clearly reluctant. But feeling sorry for the parents, who were good devotees, Sri Sankarsana das asked for the doctor to let him hold the boy. He uttered a mantra in a low tone, put the infant on his shoulder, as if to burp him, and gave him three slaps on the bottom. *Whack! Whack! Whack!* Then the baby sneezed, and started breathing again. Sri Sankarsana handed the boy back to his mother and with a gruff word not to tell anyone. The doctor made apologies and said the boy must have been in a short coma, but we all knew that Sri Sankarsana had managed it through his great devotion to Krsna and Balarama.

But Sankarsana das had a temper too, and if we saw it rarely, it was terrible when roused. Once, when an alleged Buddhist mystic from San Francisco was visiting the town near Sri Sankarsana's ashram, he tried to interfere in a gomedha sacrifice that Sankarsana das was overseeing. Three times my acarya tried to warn him away, and on the fourth time, he really lost his temper. As the American tried to drive people away and to throw dirt on the sacred fire, Sankarsana das Goswami made a spear-like mudra with his left hand, and the American Buddhist suffered an seizure on the spot. He was carried away by his devotees, and had to be hospitalized for several weeks. It was later reported that he developed epilepsy and died back in the United States, though not before sending a letter to apologize for the insult. Sri Sankarsana merely shrugged and said that if the Buddhist had been a genuine *lama*, he would have negated the mudra.

Sri Sankarsana always kept a low profile, and refused to let us publish his teachings or to bring crowds to see him. This year (2013) was the first that he allowed his disciples to even speak of him on the internet, or to receive emails on his behalf. Perhaps that should have been a sign that his time with us was drawing to an end. In the final weeks before Sri Sankarsana's disappearance this November, his disciples pleaded with him to use his powers to stay with us. He replied only that his time here was drawing to an end, and that he longed to give service to the Nagaraja in person. We could not argue with this, but we did beg permission to record his teachings while we can still remember them, and he gave us permission to publish his lessons in whatever form seems most convenient. It is my hope that another of my god-brothers, better with words, will collect these lessons and talks, and to put them together in a form that may be useful to other Vaisnava.

His Holiness Sri Sankarsana das Thakur was the most incredible acarya and mentor that I could have asked for, and his presence is deeply missed. Yet as the Bhagavad Gita teaches, this life is but a moment of *maya*, a fragment of eternity. The soul lives on, eternal and unchanging. Thus I choose to celebrate the Disappearance of my teacher, knowing that he is already closer to Lord Ananta, who is Lord Sankarsana.

PURUSHAMEDHA

I offer all glories to Sri Sankrsana das Thakur, and shares these memories and reflections, in my own poor words, in his service.

- Rudra das Goswami, 8 December 2013

PURUSHAMEDHA

V IS FOR VAISNAVA

(Parsva Ekadasi Lecture by Sri Sankarsana Das)

Today, people face a world where governments are openly corrupt, where over half the world's population starves, while 2% of the world's population gorges on over 50% of the planetary wealth. Western nations invade weaker countries to take their oil, offering empty words about 'freedom' and 'democracy', while dropping chemical weapons on urban centers, hospitals and schools. The global pollution has increased to such a disastrous extent that the polar icecaps are melting, forcing the ocean to rise at an unprecedented rate. Sickness and disease attack new communities with new viruses every day, and millions across the globe are illiterate, with no hope of improvement. The world's great religions promise salvation, while secretly profiteering off the misery of the weak and poor that they fail to protect. In short: the system is broken. The planet stagnates, physically and spiritually, edging closer to the abyss with each passing day.

But where to seek answers? Secularism has failed, leading to the decayed and inefficient governments one associates with communism and other socialist states. Science offers hope for some of the world's problems – but without the ethical or moral convictions that are derived from faith, there is little drive to pursue answers that serve the common good. We are much more likely to find technologies that benefit the very rich few, than to cure the cancer of the many poor. So people are frustrated. People are angry. They want to find answers to the very real problems that face society.

PURUSHAMEDHA

They ask: where to turn to in these dark times? Most educated or intelligent people understand that at the very best, the church/mosque/synagogue has been reduced to a pale imitation of the social institution it once was, at worst, it now serves as an active collaborator, a pacifier to convince people that "it's all going to be okay". Please, let's be honest – it is definitely NOT going to be okay!

But the question remains: if we acknowledge that faith is necessary, then how to determine which faith is best?

In this time of spiritual decay, the Gaudiya Vaisnava tradition has arisen. By Krsna's mercy, we stand apart. Bold and determined, we actively train and prepare for the coming storm that will sweep away the corruption and filth that has become the norm. Rooted fully in the 21st century, yet based in the world's most ancient and advanced spiritual sciences, we stand prepared to effect the necessary changes to light the purifying fires that will sweep across the world.

It is commonly acknowledged that the holy Vedas are the oldest and most authoritative of the world's great spiritual books. In turn the Bhagavad Gita summarizes the Vedas, and delivers the core of their teachings as follows: all of this universe, indeed all universes, are the creation of Visnu, and Visnu is the expansion of Krsna, who is the ultimate and original being. All the demigods, demons, spirits, living and unliving beings are but expansions and emanations of the original being. We too are part and parcel of Krsna, though the mortal condition blinds us to our true divine heritage.

PURUSHAMEDHA

In early ages, humanity was able to improve its condition through the performance of the complex rituals and sacrifices of the Vedas – but as the ages passed, those rituals became increasingly difficult as humanity's spiritual nature diminished. In this final age – the Kali Yuga – the highest and holiest of the demigods have abandoned the world to its ever-darkening fate. To save humanity, Krsna incarnated as the holy saint, Caitanya Mahaprabhu, in order to teach bhakti yoga (devotional living), Raganuga (extreme devotional adoration) and the practice of chanting the sacred mantra (or formula) known as the mahamantra. This mantra possesses incredible power, as if a spiritual atomic weapon, and can be used to accomplish literally anything the devotee can envision. It is intended, first and foremost, to unite the devotee with Lord Krsna. This formula is written in the Roman script as:

Hare Krsna, Hare Krsna, Krsna Krsna, Hare Hare

Hare Rama, Hare Rama, Rama Rama, Hare Hare.

The Vaisnava tradition offers a lifestyle through which the devotee can guarantee a higher rebirth, taking a place among the demigods and asuras. Through absolute and total dedication to Krsna and the discipline of the Raganuga adoration of the Supreme Lord, which is through the constant fixing of the consciousness on Krsna and the chanting of the mahamantra, the devotee is able to make spiritual progress only dreamed of in earlier yugas or ages.

PURUSHAMEDHA

The Gaudiya-Vaisnava sampradaya, a part of the greater Vaisnava tradition, acknowledges unshakeable loyalty to Lord Krsna – together with the righteous demigods and asuras. The modern Vaisnava movement also works to establish varna (social division), and seeks to guide perspective devotees to recognize and excel at their vocation as brahmans (teachers, priests), ksatriyas (warriors), vaiysas (merchants), and sudras (tradesmen).

Devotees of Lord Krsna seek to better themselves through attention to the Raganuga path, the chanting of the holy mantras, the study of the Vedas (where possible), and – most importantly – the intense worship and adoration of Lord Krsna and His expansions.

The Vaisnava path is the path of saints, lovers, criminals, and heretics – Krsna embraces all equally. The greatest devotees of Krsna include the most terrible demons, such as Vritra, Ravana, Bali *Maharaj*, and *Maya*sura. Durga and Kali are His handmaidens, and the harlot Fortune herself is His beloved mistress. Taking Lord Krsna as our spiritual master and beloved, we follow His supreme example above all others. Krsna defies all cultural norms, all taboos – He kills as He wishes, He enjoys sex as He wishes, He plays and sports as He wishes – and He teaches us, His friends and disciples to do the same. Through His incredible mercy, the most terrible sins and taboos become transformed into acts of pious devotion.

To make progress, one does not need to fast or pray or observe vigils or even perform deity worship at temple.

PURUSHAMEDHA

One needs to love Krsna madly, passionately, and to enjoy this world as part of His pastimes. Everything we do creates karma – unless we do it for Krsna, in which case there is no karma, there is only devotion. There is liberation. So if we eat meat, it is bad karma — but if we offer it to Krsna, instead it is devotion. If we kill a person then it is bad karma — but if we kill an enemy of Krsna, instead it is devotion. If we have sex with some attractive person, it is promiscuous — but if we have sex with an attractive person for Krsna, instead it is devotion. If we sacrifice an animal, maybe it is criminal — but if we sacrifice an animal (with Vedic mantras) for Krsna, it is devotion.

Remember, all things, ANYTHING, through *Hare Krsna, Hare Krsna, Krsna Krsna, Hare Hare // Hare Rama, Hare Rama, Rama Rama, Hare Hare.*

Through Krsna, we become truly liberated.

Only through Krsna, can we become truly liberated.

Jai Krsna!

हरे कृष्ण हरे कृष्ण
कृष्ण कृष्ण हरे हरे
हरे राम हरे राम
राम राम हरे हरे

PURUSHAMEDHA

VAISNAVA HALLOWEEN?

[Sri Sankarsana das Goswami, lecture October 30, 2011]

Let me speak for a moment about Halloween, and this is intended for devotees in the West.

Every year at this time, many devotees write to ask if it is permissible for their children to partake in Halloween activities.

I ask: *which* activities?

If people mean the gross promiscuity, commercialization and gluttony that is rampant Western culture, then the answer if clearly "no"! These things lead away from Lord Krsna, not towards it. But if devotees mean a focusing on the ancestors and an awareness of ancient practices of their grandparents' grandparents, then this itself is not bad. But the real devotee will show their children the real darkness that is behind Halloween and will point the children to the Lord of Darkness, who is Sri Tamasi, that is Lord Sri Rudra. And Lord Rudra is the lord of the *bhutas* (ghosts) and *piscas* (fiends) that play mischievous and naughty games at this time of year. Lord Rudra is himself Mahadev, the lord of the demigods, the most worshipful of the demigods. But Lord Rudra does not seek to be worshipped, as he is a topmost Vaisnava – He teaches the devotees to focus on the true Darkness, the Darkness that is to be feared and worshipped, and that is the real Sri Tamasi, who is Lord Krsna, the source of Lord Rudra.[1]

PURUSHAMEDHA

This time of year is very tamasic. People naturally feel a certain apprehension and respect for the darker forces. Right now, asuras and Raksasas are very powerful, and Lord Surya hides his face more and more every night. Lord Rudra and Srimate Kali love the winter months, because they have hours and hours to play and dance in the smashan grounds, ah!

Even Christians and other foreigners can sense it, which is why they developed these strange haunted festivals, to give honor to Lord Rudra and Srimate Kali.

So Vaisnava children living in asura lands – I mean the West, where many are all asuras and animals already – Vaisnava children can use Halloween to preach to the Westerners. The Western children need to see that we know the darkness better than they, but for the Vaisnava, it is not something we celebrate one night a year, and then forget. The Vaisnava loves Lord Rudra and asks Him to brings us closer to KRSNA, each and every day.

Let your children dress up as bhutas and piscas, or wrap them in a rough cloth and smear their forehead with ashes, and give them a trisul, better still. Put skull garlands around your daughters, and or let them go as Rakshasi maidens. Then when people ask you about the costumes, you have a way to explain KRSNA to them – you introduce them to Lord Rudra and Sri Kali, and then the next thing you know, you have them chanting *Hare Krsna! Hare Krsna*!

PURUSHAMEDHA

But most importantly, Lord Rudra reminds us in the Srimad Bhagavatam [SB 4.24.77-79:] of **special prayers** that can be performed, which are extremely pleasing to Lord Krsna. And we note that it is the Dark Lord, Sri Rudra (not Brahma, or Narada, or Indra) who teaches these prayers – and this is because Lord Rudra is the best devotee and most beloved of Visnu.

So certainly, let your children celebrate Halloween. But you adults, celebrate Halloween by chanting the prayers of Lord Rudra, and meditating on the teachings of the Lord of Darkness in this dark time of year.

ŚRĪ RUDRA UVĀCA:

My dear Lord, all living entities within this material world are mad after planning for things, and they are always busy with a desire to do this or that. This is due to uncontrollable greed. The greed for material enjoyment is always existing in the living entity, but Your Lordship is always alert, and in due course of time You strike him, just as a snake seizes a mouse and very easily swallows him. My dear Lord, any learned person knows that unless he worships You, his entire life is spoiled. Knowing this, how could he give up worshiping Your lotus feet? Even our father and spiritual master, Lord Brahmā, unhesitatingly worshiped You, and the fourteen Manus followed in his footsteps. My dear Lord, all actually learned persons know You as the Supreme Brahman and the Supersoul. Although the entire universe is afraid of Lord Rudra, who ultimately annihilates everything, for the learned devotees You are the fearless destination of all. [*Śrīmad Bhāgavatam* 4.24.33-68].

PURUSHAMEDHA

SACRIFICE, THE VEDAS, AND SRI PRABHUPADA

There is today a difference of opinion among modern devotees and even acaryas of the Gaudiya-Vaisnava sampradaya as to whether or not it is possible or beneficial to perform Vedic *yajnas*, in the true sense of the word where ***yajna*** implies such animal sacrifices as the classical *asvamedha* (horse sacrifice) or *gomedha* (bull sacrifice). On the one hand, the practice of animal sacrifice is clearly practiced in the Srimad Bhagavatam, even to extreme cases as *Maharaj*a Prthu, who performed almost 100 *asvamedha* rites, attracting the personal attention and manifestation of Lord Visnu. We see it echoed later in the Kali Yuga where Sri Kalki will perform the horse sacrifices for Lord Krsna, to please his father Sri Visnuyasa.

So the practice is clearly one of the utmost devotion and by the topmost Vaisnava devotees. So where does the controversy arise? Sri AC Prabhupada, the founder of ISKCON wrote about this topic in several of his books. On the one hand, when speaking in public, he seemed against the sacrificial *yajnas*. His commentaries, however, tell a different story. While he and Sankarsana das disagree on whether or not such practices should be practiced today, they seem to agree that they must only be performed by a brahmana who is trained and qualified to carry out the Vedic instructions for the ritual.

PURUSHAMEDHA

That is to say that Prabhupada acknowledged that he was not trained to do the *yajna* sacrifices, and thus very rightly he instructed his American devotees to avoid such sacrifices. This deviation from Indian Vaisnava practice is permitted, because as the *Srimad Bhagavtam* makes clear, it is a sin for the priest to perform the sacrifice if he is unqualified.

However, many American and European devotees believe incorrectly that Sri Prabhupada denied the Vedic practice entirely. This is not at all the case, as the many sections of Prabhupada's commentary on the Srimad Bhagavatam makes plain. Prabhupada clearly distinguished that animal sacrifice was ordained in the Vedas, and that it has auspicious benefits. Sri Lalita Thakur practiced the *yajnas*, as do other contemporary acaryas, such as Sri Sankarsana das.

For the benefit of devotees who follow Sri Prabhupada's teachings, these following of his quotations are shared [Editor's note: these follow the edition on Bhaktivedanta Vedabase]:

'Aśvamedha yajñas or gomedha yajñas, sacrifices in which a horse or a bull is sacrificed, were not, of course, for the purpose of killing the animals. Lord Caitanya said that such animals sacrificed on the altar of yajña were rejuvenated and a new life was given to them. It was just to prove the efficacy of the hymns of the Vedas. By recitation of the hymns of the Vedas in the proper way, certainly the performer gets relief from the reactions of sins, but in case of such sacrifices improperly done under inexpert

PURUSHAMEDHA

management, surely one has to become responsible for animal sacrifice.' (**Prabhupada's Commentary — 1, Ch 8, v.52**)

"Nārada Muni wanted to draw King Prācīnabarhiṣat's attention to the excesses of killing animals in sacrifices. It is said in the śāstras that by killing animals in a sacrifice, one immediately promotes them to human birth. Similarly, by killing their enemies on a battlefield, the kṣatriyas who fight for a right cause are elevated to the heavenly planets after death. In Manu-saṁhitā it is stated that it is necessary for a king to execute a murderer so that the murderer will not suffer for his criminal actions in his next life." (**Prabhupada's Commentary – 4.25.9**)

"With great faith King Bharata performed various kinds of sacrifice. He performed the sacrifices known as agni-hotra, darśa, pūrṇamāsa, cāturmāsya, paśu-yajña [wherein a horse is sacrificed] and soma-yajña [wherein a kind of beverage is offered]. Sometimes these sacrifices were performed completely and sometimes partially. In any case, in all the sacrifices the regulations of cāturhotra were strictly followed. In this way Bharata Mahārāja worshiped the Supreme Personality of Godhead.*" PURPORT: *Animals like hogs and cows were offered in sacrifice to test the proper execution of the sacrifice. Otherwise, there was no purpose in killing the animal. Actually the animal was offered in the sacrificial fire to get a rejuvenated life. Generally an old animal was sacrificed in the fire. and it would come out again in a youthful body.* (**Prabhupada's Commentary – 5.7.5**)

PURUSHAMEDHA

Thus it is clear that even while acarya Prabhupada did not practice sacrifices, his commentaries do not deny the practice, which the great teacher could not and would not have done in good faith, as he observed such practices in India. Devotees who desire to engage in sacrificial practices should not be hasty to do so on their own, as the rites and mantras are very precise. Yet neither should devotees shun opportunities to attend and participate in *yajnas*, as the Lord delights *yajnas*, **and is Himself the yajna**, as He informs us in the Bhagavad Gita. Rather, sincere Vaisnava are eager to partake in *yajnas* wherever possible, when overseen by properly trained brahmana who have learned the correct Vedic mantras.

PURUSHAMEDHA

CONTEMPORARY VEDIC WORSHIP AND SACRIFICE

(*"Navatri Notes"*, October 2013)

SB 3.29.38: "Lord Viṣṇu, the Supreme Personality of Godhead, who is the enjoyer of all sacrifices, is the time factor and the master of all masters. He enters everyone's heart, He is the support of everyone, and He causes every being to be annihilated by another."

Srimate Bhavani street puja in Dhaka slums (inner city)

The photos are taken from Srimate Bhavani street puja in Dhaka. In very poor areas of the city, brahmanas must conduct Vedic rites using very simple implements. Sri Sankarsana Das reminds us frequently that **when offered** correctly in accordance with the Vedas, sacrifice benefits three parties.

- **First**, the benefactor or provider of the sacrifice is blessed by Lord Visnu and the demigods, for providing the offering.
- **Second,** the brahmana is blessed by conducting the sacrificial rites in accordance with the Vedas.
- **Third,** the animal itself benefits from the sacrifice, by being immediately promoted to an excellent rebirth, even with the possibility of rebirth on Satyaloka or Brahmaloka.

It is also important to note that the meat of the sacrifices is given as prasadam afterwards to the poor, who benefit from partaking in the Lord's auspicious leavings.

Srimate Bhavani street puja in Dhaka (inner city)

PURUSHAMEDHA

The Lord says in the Srimad Bhagvatam: [SB 2.3.8-9:] "One should worship Lord Vishnu or His devotee for spiritual advancement in knowledge, and for protection of heredity and advancement of a dynasty one should worship the various demigods. One who desires domination over a kingdom or an empire should worship the Manus. One who desires victory over an enemy should worship the demons, and one who desires sense gratification should worship the moon. But one who desires nothing of material enjoyment should worship the Supreme Personality of Godhead."

So it is clear that classic Vaisnava scriptures make clear that worship of the demigods and asuras is indeed recommended for various purposes, so Vaisnava should indeed celebrate Navratri and similar feast days honoring the demigods. Nevertheless, all sacrifices are ultimately enjoyed by Lord Krsna Himself, the Supreme Personality of Godhead, of Whom the demigods and asuras are mere expansions of expansions.

PURUSHAMEDHA

THE PRACTICE OF INTERNAL WORSHIP
(Sri Sankarsana Das Goswami, 9 October lecture)

Many Vaisnava today have forgotten the joys of celebrated pujas daily in the house and in the temple. Some devotees, even brahmanas, write to me that they are upset not to have such nice temples as we have in Vrindavan. They say, "Oh Gurudev, I would do nice pujas if only I had a nice temple", and other such excuses. Well this is flawed thinking, and I want to explain this clearly, so as to remove their excuses and prevent them from further offending the Lord's holy presence, ah.

Look, we know already from the holy Vedas and Puranas that this world is entirely *maya*. The temple, the implements of worship, the conch, the bells, the plates – all *maya*. All of it. They are lovely toys to make pujas, but they are no more real or solid to Lord Krsna than the same ones that you can imagine in your mind's eye. Sri Prabhupada, the student of my acarya's brother, wrote this in two of his books: "In this connection there is a story about a brāhmaṇa who was offering sweet rice to the Lord within his mind. The brāhmaṇa had no money nor any means of worshiping the Deity, but within his mind he arranged everything nicely. He had gold pots to bring water from the sacred rivers to wash the Deity, and he offered the Deity very sumptuous food, including sweet rice. Once, before he offered the sweet rice, he thought that it was too hot, and he thought, "Oh, let me test it. My, it is very hot." When he put his finger in the sweet rice to test it, his finger was burned and his meditation broken. Although he was offering food to the

PURUSHAMEDHA

Lord within his mind, the Lord accepted it nonetheless. Consequently, the Lord in Vaikuṇṭha immediately sent a chariot to bring the brāhmaṇa back home, back to Godhead."

Well, my acarya (Sri Lalita Thakura) used to tell one other story that Sri Prabhupada did not tell, though he knew it also. There was a holy brahmana, some years ago when the Christians were in power in Kerala, who was very devoted to Lord Narasimha. He would undertake great austerities and penances to draw closer to the Lord, and was very much respected by other brahmanas. Unfortunately, the British governor resented this man for his status in the community, and so he would send his soldiers to harass the holy man at night. They would do mischief – befoul his house walls with urine, through excrement over the walls, vile behavior. They would smash bottles of wine against the windows, anything they could do to make him feel badly. And this holy man, he endured it all with great joy, since he was happy to suffer for Lord Narasimha. But one day the soldiers harassed the daughter of the brahman, and this was too much. So he performed the holy purushamedha in his mind, with great concentration and dedication to the Lord. He visualized every detail: the offerings, libations, sacrifices, the mantras, and he visualized the governor and his Christian soldiers lashed to the sacrificial stakes. He imaged them burning in the ritual fires, screaming as they burned, as he chanted the mantras to Lord Agni, Lord Varuna, and Lord Visnu. He concentrated so hard that he could smell their flesh cooking.

PURUSHAMEDHA

And when he was with finished the puja, he fell into a deep sleep and slept very soundly.

Well, in the morning, there was absolute chaos in the streets. When the sudra ladies came to do service, they told his wife that in the night, the governor had been hosting a party for his officers. Somehow, and it was not clear, they had all had a great deal of wine to drink (as Christians do, even their priests), and some debauchery had led to a fire in the kitchens. It spread with remarkable fury throughout the house, and the governor and his men were too drunk to escape. The ladies of the house escaped, as did the servants, but they were unable to get to the governor or his officers, who perished — screaming in horror. Worst of all, the servants swore that they could hear a spirit intoning Vedic mantras over the roar of the flames. When the fires died down, the bodies were burned entirely to ash, consumed by the fires.

And after that, of course, no one dared to trouble the holy brahmana again, and his family was respected doubly for his sanctity and piety thereafter. And the governor and his men, it can be said safely, passed to Vaikuntha, as they received liberation through their sacrifice in the purushamedha ritual, which was correctly celebrated by the holy Vaisnava devotee.

This story, explained my acarya Sri Lalita Thakur, needs to be told along with Sri Prabhupada's account, in order for devotees to fully understand the impact of puja. That is to say that when a devotee undertakes spiritual exercises with great intention and concentration, the results cannot and should not be underestimated. So we must be very careful how and when we visualize the Lord, and not cause some offence to Him (in any of his forms) through bad attention or wandering thoughts. Rather, we should fix our attention on Him, controlling the senses, with full knowledge that He accepts our inner and outer devotions with equal pleasure. I say again: He accepts our inner and outer worship with equal devotion.

So I encourage those devotees: do not make excuses! Chant the holy names with fervor and devotion, but make time also to celebrate the Lord with attention and detail. The Lord delights in the devotee who pays Him attention, and there is no higher service than the Lord's pleasure.

Remember, all things, ANYTHING, through *Hare Krsna, Hare Krsna, Krsna Krsna, Hare Hare // Hare Rama, Hare Rama, Rama Rama, Hare Hare.*

Through Krsna, we become truly liberated.

Only through Krsna, can we become truly liberated.

Jai Krsna!

PURUSHAMEDHA

KNOWING THE GUNAS

(Indira Ekadasi 2010 lecture by Sri Sankarsana das)

It is stated clearly in the Vedas that material nature (prakṛti) is of three qualities, namely Sattva (being or purity), Rajas (passion), and Tamas (darkness). Everything material in the world is aligned with one of the three gunas, and every living being in the material world, by Krsna's mercy, possesses these attributes in different measure. Now this is material nature, Krsna's *maya* made manifest. Krsna Himself is beyond the three gunas, which He reminds us in the Sri Bhagavad Gita saying:

tribhirguṇamayairbhāvairebhiḥ sarvamidaṁ jagat |
mohitaṁ nābhijānāti māmebhyaḥ paramavyayam | |
7.13| |

The World deluded by these Three Gunas does not know Me: Who is beyond these Gunas and imperishable. (7.13)

Now in the Vedic literature and especially in the earlier yugas, it was understood that these gunas are gifts of Krsna through His *maya*, they were not a trap or a punishment. They were part of the system or game He designed for his amusement. There was no thinking that sattva is good and tamas is evil – that kind of thinking comes from Christian missionaries in Kerala, it's not Vedic at all. Krsna Himself designed the universe according to these qualities, which He himself is beyond, but He does not intend for us to be beyond them as long as we take birth in the Kali Yuga. Take

Lord Siva, for example. We read in the Vedic literatures that He is Mahadeva and Sri Bhagavan – the Master of the Demigods. And yet Lord Krsna calls Lord Siva by the name 'Tamasi', meaning the divinity of tamas (darkness). And this is not an insult, for Sri Krsna loves Lord Siva very dearly, and Lord Siva is the greatest of the demigods and the best Vaisnava. Lord Siva is the most tamasic being in the entire universe, but he is not deluded or lethargic (the way some books would have you believe), but possessor of the darker and frightening energies of material creation. This is why ghosts and goblins dance in His train.

A counter-example: Indra is sometimes called the king of the demigods too, and so he is very sattvic, because the devas are sattvic by nature. But this does not mean that He was a good devotee, and in fact, his greatest enemies were very tamasic beings who were better Vaisnavas than Him! Lord Vrtrasura was a very great Brahmin who allows Lord Indra to kill him as a type of purushamedha, and Bali *Maharaj*a was such a great devotee of Visnu that he defeated Indra utterly and humbled him. And Bali *Maharaj*a was entirely tamasic, and lord of the asuras, who are completely tamasic beings. He was the greatest Vaisnava of his age, and even now he rules a kingdom with Lord Vamana as his doorkeeper. So we can see that the Vedic literatures do not distinguish one guna as better than another, it's just not there.

In fact, we see that it is the rajasic and tamasic beings that tend to take on the really severe penances to please the Lord. Ravana and Hiranyakashipu are two very serious devotees,

PURUSHAMEDHA

and they earned the direct attention of the Lord Himself. They are tamasic to the core, and they received liberation. But the demigods like Indra, they reach the heavenly planets and stop there – their sattva is a hindrance, not an asset. So we can see clearly that no guna is better than another guna, they are just innate characteristics that need to be harnessed appropriately.

And here, we are reminded that transcendental qualities are sometimes like material qualities for the sake of comparison, but that they are not the same. Krsna and Radha enjoy lust and sexual pleasure – this is clear – but it is a different type of sexual pleasure, a transcendental lust. The Srimad Bhagavatam uses erotic language to stimulate your rajasic qualities, but this is to help you reach the real rajas, the a-rajas (transcendental rajas) of the Vaikuntha planets. You begin with the material rajas, and it helps you to discover the real rajas. The same for sattva and tamas – the forms we experience here are not the same as the devatas and asuras, and even their experience is not the same as Lord Brahma or Lord Sankarsana. And Krsna's transcendental qualities, well you already know, they are entirely beyond anything I can describe in language.

I am telling you this today because we do have some recent swamis and charlatans who lie to devotees and tell them that they need to be sattvic, that only sattvic devotees can earn Krsna's favor. They tell you that you must abstain from meat, not drink coffee, and not look too closely at a pretty boy or girl. Jai Krsna, what nonsense! What an offence against the Lord! Are these fake swamis even reading the

PURUSHAMEDHA

Vedas? One only needs to look at great devotees like my mahacarya, Sri Bhaktivinoda Thakur, who was a dedicated Vaisnava, a householder, a meat-eater, a tea drinker, and we can see that this new idea of the puritan regulative principles is absolute hogwash. It comes from the British Christians in Kerala. It has no basis in Vaisnava practice, and many excellent brahmanas and sannyasis of the Vaisnava sampradaya have never shied away from coffee or tea or some fish. And this is known in India, this isn't a secret – but we have these new devotees coming to us from America and trying to teach us to be Hindu.

So I tell you like I tell all my students: know your guna, and make it work for you. If you are sattvic, Jai Krsna! Then follow sattvic devotions and disciplines. If you are rajasic, Jai Krsna! Then be aggressive, fiery in your austerities. If you are tamasic, Jai Krsna! You have the greatest Vaisnava as role-models, so follow their example and please the Lord. If you are sattvic like a devata, then be a devata, if you are tamasic like an asura, then be an asura. But don't pretend to be what you are not, because then you will surely fail. You cannot overcome your own nature which Krsna and karma have assigned you. Like Krsna told Arjuna on the battlefield: know your role and play it! But if you can identify your guna and your varna (that's another lesson for another day), then you have some real clues on how to better serve the lotus feet of the Lord – and exactly as He expects you to.

PURUSHAMEDHA

Remember, all things, ANYTHING, through *Hare Krsna, Hare Krsna, Krsna Krsna, Hare Hare // Hare Rama, Hare Rama, Rama Rama, Hare Hare.*

Through Krsna, we become truly liberated.

Only through Krsna, can we become truly liberated.

Jai Krsna!

हरे कृष्ण हरे कृष्ण
कृष्ण कृष्ण हरे हरे
हरे राम हरे राम
राम राम हरे हरे

PURUSHAMEDHA

UNLIMITED POWER

(21 September Lecture 2011 by Sri Sankarsana Das)

"Many devotees, especially Europeans and Americans, come to India and want to discover the secrets of yoga, tantric powers, magical siddhis. And they go to all these supposed gurus, who give them very light austerities and ask for money. Lots of money, you know? So these Americans, these Westerners, they give the money, and they get some little secrets of yoga, and they go back to the West and open a studio and teach their little secret, and they charge more money. And what does this get? Karma. Karma for the guru who charged money, karma for the Westerner who paid the money, karma for the students who pay money to go to the new studio to learn the little secrets. Ah. And it's really all for nothing, it's for little siddhis that aren't worth even as much as a book or a cell phone today.

Listen, I will tell you a real secret. If you want power, real power, power like Vrtrasura, Narada Muni, Arjuna, *Maya*sura, Bali *Maharaj*, or Lord Ravana, you only need one secret, one practice. It is a mantra, a mantra that can give you literally anything you want, anything you need. Ah. Listen carefully, here is the mantra:

HARE KRSNA HARE KRSNA // KRSNA KRSNA HARE HARE HARE RAMA HARE RAMA // RAMA RAMA HARE HARE.

You fix your intention or your goal in your mind, and then you chant this mantra, at least 1728 times per day.

PURUSHAMEDHA

If you are impatient, you want to make real progress very quickly, you chant it 6912 times per day. But that is a severe austerity, that takes real dedication, I don't think anyone has it today.

When I was young, I wanted to be an aghori, to do terrible rites, and sleep in the smashan, and have an asuri or raksasi for a — you know — for a wife, and to get a lot of money and power. In other words, I wanted to be a Westerner, because they do terrible things, and their women are all raksasis, and they have a lot of money and power, ah?

But my acarya Sri Lalita das Thakur, he told me: "Prabhu, you chant this mantra, and you will not be sorry. You will get the asuri, you will get the money, but you don't need those things. Krsna is what you need, and Krsna will give you all the wonderful, terrible things you need. But when you get them, you won't want them, you will just want Krsna". And I trusted my acarya, and he was not wrong at all.

So today I am telling you: you want to have supernatural dreams and visions? Chant HARE KRSNA. You want to be with an asuri or asura? Chant HARE KRSNA. You want to travel to different planets and see spirits and get powers? Chant HARE KRSNA. You want to end global warming, or make the Yuga end faster? Chant HARE KRSNA. You can get anything, anything by chanting HARE KRSNA.

But when you do chant HARE KRSNA, you will find eventually that all those things don't matter – only Sri Krsna matters, only serving Him and being His friend and servant. Then those other things are just pastimes, they are amusements for you and Krsna to enjoy – but the real joy is Krsna himself.

Remember, all things, ANYTHING, through *Hare Krsna, Hare Krsna, Krsna Krsna, Hare Hare // Hare Rama, Hare Rama, Rama Rama, Hare Hare.*

Through Krsna, we become truly liberated.

Only through Krsna, can we become truly liberated.

Jai Krsna!

हरे कृष्ण हरे कृष्ण
कृष्ण कृष्ण हरे हरे
हरे राम हरे राम
राम राम हरे हरे

PURUSHAMEDHA

A MEDITATION ON RADHA FOR THE KALI YUGA

Jai Radha-Krsna! All glories to our master, Srila Sankarsana das Goswami, who benefitted from the mercy of Srila Lalita Prasad Thakur. All glories to the great teacher of the last century, the reviver of the Vaisnava sampradaya, the teacher of the harinam and sankirtana, Srila Bhaktivinoda Thakura. We take refuge at their lotus feet, and beseech them to bring us to Krsna.

Srila Sankarsana remarks often that it is lamentable today to see how distorted the Vaisnava sampradaya has become, especially in its offshoots in lands outside of India. Many well-meaning devotees give up their lands, their wives, their wealth and their children, and sincerely embark on a quest to learn find Krsna in the Vedas and the Puranas, and fall prey to those gurus who misguide the unwary. Some of the worst of these gurus have even gone so far as to deny or deliberately misinterpret the teachings of the great acaryas of the past.

Our beloved master, the great of this age, Sri Bhaktivinoda Thakura, taught his sons that there are many paths to Krsna (like jnana, bhakti, ragunaga). The lesser of these paths is for the spiritually weaker and for mleccas, which is the path of bhakti through austerity and renunciation out of fear of Krsna. The greater of these paths is ragunaga-bhakti, which is the path of pure devotion through love for Krsna. When the Vaisnava sampradaya came to America and

PURUSHAMEDHA

England, Prabhupada (the disciple of Sri Bhaktivinoda Thakura's son) taught the Yankees the regulative principles, some little Sanskrit, some simple pujas, and this was very correct. Yet when he returned to India, he had almost forgotten entirely that this path is merely the beginning of the Vedas and the Puranas, and not its sum.

Srila Lalita Thakur often reminded Srila Sankarsana das Goswami that a close reading of the Bhagavad Gita, the Srimad Bhagvatam, and the Vedas all teaches the same cosmic truth: Krsna is supreme. Moreover, there is no contradiction between them: one cannot say 'oh, the ashmavedha and purushamedha were very good in the Satya Yuga or Treta Yuga, but not today', because this denies the holy Vedas, which is to deny Krsna. So we cannot deny the Veda or try to hide it, but rather we must hold to it, because the Vedas are Krsna's eternal words, and the Bhagavad Gita is the heart of the Vedas.

Today, Sri Sankarsana das Goswami instructs us that we must both live according to the Vedas, but in a way that acknowledges the Kali Yuga. How can we do this? We can do so, Gududev teaches, by correctly understanding the Vedas and the Bhagavad Gita in the light of the Kali Yuga. As an example, Sattva, Rajas, and Tamas are the three gunas. In Sanskrit and Hindi, the meaning is very clear. But in English, people translate 'tamas' as 'ignorance', and this is entirely wrong. *Tamas* is darkness, and this is why Lord Mahadev Siva is called Sri Tamasi – because he is the Lord of Darkness. Darkness conceals, and in this way it is correct that it conceals the divine self and causes the ego. But ignorance is a product of Darkness, not Darkness itself. In Sanskrit, one cannot make this mistake. But when we read English translations of the holy books, we are disheartened by these errors. It is like someone threw out the dictionary!

Lord Mahadeva is the Lord of Darkness, and in this capacity He takes on tamasic beings like ghosts, asuras, and raksasas as his disciples and playmates. In this role, He takes Mahakali as His consort, and He spends time in tamasic places like the graveyard and crematorium. Lord Siva kills brahmans and dances among corpses, He eats meat, He smokes intoxicants, He has illegal relations with Mohini, beasts, and with some asuris. Lord Mahadev meditates on the aspect of Krsna that is the Transcendent Darkness, Lord Sankarsana, who resides beneath the Universe. When we read about Lord Sankarsana and Lord Shiva, we cannot see Ignorance, but rather the Darkness, the true Darkness. To somehow connect the effects of *tamas* (Darkness) with *ajnana* (ignorance) is a great error and a great sin against Lord Tamasi. Is Sri Tamasi "the ignorant one"? What a blasphemy! And Lord Siva is the greatest Vaisnava, and He is even the founder of the Rudra sampradaya, which is part of the Gaudiya-Vaisnava sampradaya.

Sri Sankarasana Goswami reminds us that since we are living in the Kali Yuga, then we are in the Age (*yuga*) of Darkness (*kali*). And we need to understand this, to practice the sanatana dharma in a way that is effective today. In the age of Darkness, we need to be willing to perform extremes of austerity to gain the same benedictions that were easy to gain in the earlier yugas. And Krsna Himself provides the supreme examples of this. We should learn from true devotees like Sri Ravana, Sri *Maya*sura, Sri Mahabali, who were such excellent devotees that they received the Lord's personal attentions – and yet they were entirely in the mode of tamas. One could not be possibly more tamasic! And this is the mode that is called for in the Kali Yuga. And surely the greatest of all devotees in the former age was surely Srimate Radha and her companions, who practiced perfect Krsna consciousness, in a fully Vedic manner, but in the mode of Darkness, that is to say in a way that appeared illicitly, in a way that would have scandalized the prudish Vaisnava of today. Their seeming madness and longing for Krsna was not one of ignorance, nor of sattvic or rajasic modes, but one of utter defiance of the norms and taboos of the day. Krsna consciousness – without limits!

Above all, we should fix our minds fully on Krsna, and be always conscious of doing all things (sattvic, rajasic, or tamasic) for Krsna. If we are genuinely practicing the highest path of love, that is raganuga-bhakti – then by dedicating even the most terrible acts to Him (as Arjuna on the battlefield), or the most illict acts (like Lalita and Radha did with Krsna in the forest) one purifies the act and is rescued from the consequences by the mercy of the Lord himself.

This is our best efforts to present the teachings of Sri Sankarasana das Goswami, and we beg his mercy and forgiveness for the many errors therein.

Hare Krsna!

PURUSHAMEDHA

ASVAMEDHA

Sankarsana das did not have many disciples. He preferred not to take too many students, because (he said) a guru with many disciples is really a guru with no disciples. When we made the odd trip into Vrindavan to visit the temples, he would get really cross when he'd see foreign swamis with huge crowds of initiates following them. "This is not Vedic," he would growl. "Look, in *Mahabharata*, when Arjuna and his brothers go to study with their guru, are they among one hundred other students? No, the guru takes four or five students at a time, ten at the most, and makes them his focus. But these damn Yankees," (and he'd wave at a saffron robed fellow), "they tell people to follow them and that they will take on their karmas – but that's not Vedic at all! No one can take on your karmas, the best that they can do is give you some attention and help you overcome your own karmas. If gurus could take on the karmas of the world, then how the hell did the British colonize India? These Americans collect devotees like a child collects baseball cards or marbles, it is just a game for their own egos. Worse, they ask for *dakshina* for the privilege of following them. What a disgrace, and it offends Krsna. Do not think it will go unpunished – it will not go unpunished."

But that is not to say that he did not have any disciples. He did have a few loyal students, like my old friend Ramkrsna das, and others that would occasionally visit him to ask his blessing or his help, or sometimes just his advice. On one particular afternoon, when nothing special was happening, we heard a car rumbling along the muddy road which led to Sankarsana's small home. Soon, through the trees, you could see a very expensive silver Cadillac coming towards us. I did not know the license plates of India very well back then, but one of my godsisters told me afterwards that the car was from Mumbai. The car parked, and the driver got out and opened the passenger door. First, an incredibly stout man emerged from the car, with all the ponderous dignity of a man of great importance. He was almost bald, and looked to be about the same age as Sankarsana. A strikingly pretty younger woman, who cannot have been more than mid-twenties, followed him. I assumed she was his daughter, but later afterwards learned that she was his wife. The door of the house opened, and my guru stepped out into the sunlight, squinting against the sun's glare. When he saw the guests who were making their way towards him, a broad smile played across his face. He looked genuinely happy to see them, and barked out a gruff welcome to the old gent. The gent boomed out a reply, and moved to embrace Sankarsana. My guru seized his guest, very warmly, and he acknowledged the pranams of the younger lady with the usual near-embarrassment with which he accepted the due obeisances. Shows of fawning deference always made him uncomfortable, as he insisted such displays were a medieval Muslim custom, and not native to Vedic culture. It was clear that the lady did not know whether to bow or to shake hands, but Sankarsana quickly moved to take her hand and ushered them into the house, calling for the devotees to bring tea and refreshments.

PURUSHAMEDHA

Sankarsana did not invite his students into the house to visit with the guests, and once the refreshments were brought for the guests, the devotees were sent out of the building also. The guests cannot have stayed more than an hour, which I found surprising, as the drive cannot have been a short one. Before the guests left, the old gent had the driver bring several packages from the back of the car, and I distinctly recall one of them being a good-sized crate of expensive brandy. Sankarsana accepted these gifts with a very grave demeanor. The gent appeared to be very grateful for whatever conversation had taken place, and he was practically chortling as he made his way back to the car – and he even gave the young lady a playful pat on her rear!

Sankarsana gave an amused snort as the gent began to ponderously lower himself into the car, and he turned to me and winked.

"Those people, they are horse-fuckers!" he smirked.

Needless to say, I was a bit taken off guard by this particular expression.

"Sorry, what's that?" I asked.

"I mean that they are very rich. Oh, he is very successful. Big business man, he has a lot of money. Nice house, nice car, very pretty wife. She is greedy like him, she married him for his money. She has a boyfriend, I think, but her husband does not really care, as long as she is discreet. They are very attached to this world, and so he asks Lord Krsna and Lord Siva to give him material success. Well, he has been my student for a long time, and I despair of him reaching moksha, but I can at least help them get some nice things here and now."

"But why did you call them both horse-fuckers?" I asked in a puzzled tone.

"Jai Krsna, you are very young," growled my guru in an amused tone. "You tell me – what is the *Asvamedha*?"

That much I knew. "The *Asvamedha* is the Vedic horse sacrifice, which is performed for kings and princes that wish to make their kingdom legitimate. It is only rarely performed today, as it's said to be complex."

PURUSHAMEDHA

"Oh, it is complex, it is complex – but how do they sacrifice the horse?" my teacher asked quizzically.

This I did not know, I admitted.

He chuckled, in that sordid way he sometimes affected.

"The ceremony took a year and three days. For one year, a white stallion had to roam freely throughout a territory. So they had to protect the animal from thieves and robbers. Some sages say that the horse was a symbol, that it used to be a prince instead, but that is just hearsay. After the year had passed, there was the sacrifice ceremony. On the second day of the ceremony, the raj would ride in his chariot, pulled by the stallion and other horses. Then the wives of the raj would anoint the stallion with musk, on the head, the flanks, and the phallus, as if it was getting married. Some texts say that they had to massage the phallus to excite the stallion. The attendants would put up a tent, like for a wedding, and the chief queen was dressed as if for a wedding. Then the stallion was smothered with silk curtains, because you did not want to harm the horse or wound it, it has to be perfect. Then, while the stallion was still warm and erect, the queen had to fondle it and mount it, calling it her husband."

"You are not suggested that she actually – ah – that she fucked the horse?" I asked, understandably horrified.

"Oh, she fucked the horse. She fucked the horse very good. The ritual demands it."

PURUSHAMEDHA

I refused to believe it, of course. So he brought me inside, and pulled two books from his dusty shelves where he kept the White and Black Vedas.

"This is the *Apastamba Srauta Sutra* and this is *Taittiriya Samhita*, they are part of the Vedas. Not 'Vedic literatures' like those fake swamis say – these are the real Vedas from Vyasa."

He searched for a passage and passed me the *Taittiriya Samhita*.

"Can you read the Sanskrit?" he asked.

At that point, I could make out a few words, but some of them were not familiar. He scanned the page, and started reading in Sanskrit, with his deep, rich voice:

> *krsyai tva ksemaya tva*
> *rayyaf tva pdsaya tva*
> *prthivyai tva ntariksaya tva dive tva*
> *sate tva sate tva*

Then in English, he translated:

> You for ploughing, you for inhabiting,
> You for riches, you for increase,
> You for earth, you for air, you for heaven,
> You for existence, you for the void.

And then more:

PURUSHAMEDHA

vasubhir devebhir devataya
gayatrena tva chandasa yunajmi
vasantena tvartuna havisa dlksayami

As the devas being deity,
As the gayatri being the meter, I yoke you,
As the spring the being oblation, I consecrate you,

"The Queen, she is talking to the horse while she is rubbing him with nice musk. She is telling him why they are going to sacrifice him, and telling the listeners too. But that is not where it stops."

He started to chuckle. "Then she starts to talk dirty to the stallion, she tells him it is time for fucking. Oh! you don't believe me? Well the Vedas read:

> *a'ham ajani garbhadham a tvam ajasi garbadham*
> *tau saha caturah padah sam pra sarayavahai.*

Which means:

> Come on, stallion! Mate with me, you stud! I'm asking you sweetly for mating: let the two of us get busy and entwine our limbs.

And after she says this, in case there is any doubt left, the pujari (priest says):

> *ut sakthyor grdam dhehi*
> *anjim udanjim anv aja*

PURUSHAMEDHA

ya striram jivabhojano
ya asam biladhavanah
priya strinam apicyah
ya asam krsne laksmani
sardigrdim paravadhit.

In English, it means:

> Bring the cock betwixt the thighs,
> drive along the erect and wet one
> which is women's live pleasure,
> which is their penetration,
> women's deep secret
> which has hit the clitoris,
> in the dark-haired cleft.

"Then," he concluded, "they would butcher the stallion and offer the meat and blood to the sacred fire, like any yajna."

"And the queen?" I asked in a quavering voice, expecting the worst.

"Oh, she was probably sore for a few days, and the *raj* would have fucked her good and hard as soon as the ritual was over, in hopes of begetting a strong prince on her."

I must have looked appalled, and Sankarsana just started laughing and laughing. "Oh, you Americans!" he barked. "You think religion is all prudish. What is wrong with you? Religion is dirty and sordid, and Krsna is dirty and sordid

PURUSHAMEDHA

too. Why, didn't you see his name in there? *ya asam* **krsne laksmani** – It is figuratively Sanskrit for "women's pleasure", but it is literally *Laksmi's Krsna*. You see? Krsna is in the Vedas, but you have to read the dirty parts with horse-fucking to find him. Oh Krsna, you are a naughty boy!" He started to laugh again, so hard that he began to cough and turn red.

When he finally calmed down, he told me sit down on the couch. He put the books back on the shelf, and he told me to get two glasses from the kitchen. I did so, and when I came back, he had opened a bottle of the brandy which the gent had brought.

"*Maharaj*, I understand that the ritual is nasty, but what does that have to do with your guest and his wife?"

He frowned at me. "Didn't you hear anything I just explained? He is a *raj*, she is a queen."

Ugh. I was aghast.

"You are not suggesting," I said slowly, "that they actually performed the *asvamedha*."

"Why not?" he asked, "is it not in the Vedas?"

"Well yes, but she actually fucked a horse?"

"Oh she did. He did too, he fucked a young mare, the dirty fellow. You see that in the Vedic commentaries as a supplementary practice to the main rite, while they are butchering the stallion afterwards."

"But who would even perform that ritual today?" I asked, and I confess I was morbidly curious.

"Oh, son, listen to me carefully. All joking aside, this ritual is in the Vedas. It is a holy rite, it is sastra – do you not understand? It is not dirty, it is a terribly sacred thing. The only ritual as holy is the *purushamedha*, and you have heard me speak about this already. Listen, when Lord Kalki comes, he will perform the asvamedha himself. Let me be clear, and do not misunderstand me: Lord Kalki will have his wives sexually caress a stallion, and he will expect his wife to fondle its cock and mount it for hard sex. It will happen, and that is sastra. That is the dharma. Visnu might order us to do things that are transgressive, but that is only because we do not properly understand the significance."

"So that older fellow, he actually had a horse roam for an entire year, and then had that – that ritual performed for him?"

"Yes," said Sankarsana very soberly, "and I assisted at the rite, though the main pujari was a well-respected fellow from Mumbai."

"But the cost?"

"Immense," he admitted.

PURUSHAMEDHA

"So why?" I asked.

"Gold breeds gold," he intoned, as if it were a proverb. "Look, he spent a great deal of money to sponsor the ritual five years ago, and he was almost a millionaire then. Today he is a multimillionaire, and he might become a billionaire. Who knows?" He shrugged. "I feel badly for him, though, since this is not what I would have liked for him."

"But you are always saying "*artha, dharma, kama, moksha*," I said, "and *artha* is wealth."

"Artha is wealth, and artha is good," he said, "and besides, Laksmi is wealth. Krsna is married to wealth. But Krsna does not want us to lose sight of Him in our quest for wealth. I worry that this fellow has gotten so fond of his gold that he no longer cares if his pretty wife is fucking her boyfriend. That is not proper kama, and there are bad karmas in play. But I am trying to get them back on the right path. At least the asvamedha will have removed some bad karmas tied to the artha, and there may be hope for him yet. I will never give up on any of my students, even the bad ones." He chuckled. "And I have a lot of bad ones!"

He slapped me affectionately, and I did not protest too much.

"What should you learn? Clearly, religion is not the clear-cut system of public performance that we often take it to be. Religion – and I mean Vedic religion – is and always has been a dark business. Real ritual is transgressive, in that it violates the boundaries of *maya*. If ritual feels mundane, then it is just play-acting. But speaking honestly – and I mean genuinely very directly and simply – the Vedic rites are all very terrifying. That fellow – when he saw his wife splayed across the belly of the stallion, and its cock making its way into her womb, do you think he felt normal? No, he will never forget. And how do you think he felt when he had to mount a mare? When he put his organ into its yoni? I can't imagine, but he was probably terrified. They will never forget that day. Never. Not until they die. That ritual changed them as people, they could never again make love without thinking about that sacrifice. You see, it's not the horse that suffered, it was them. By fucking horses, they gave up part of their humanity, and joined themselves to the world of beasts and asuras. In that moment that they experienced orgasm (and the text says that they have to), they were almost rakshasas. Neither man nor beast, understand? So when you do sacrifice, look for the hidden cost."

"But does it work?" I insisted.

"Oh, Jai Krsna, yes of course. Look, Visnu does not give false rites in the Veda. The shastra is very clear: he who performs the ritual shall have the cosmos recognize their sovereignty. Do you see? If someone undergoes that rite, then the universe itself has to adjust to recognize that those people are not normal people like you or me – those people are really kings and queens, and so the universe will treat them accordingly.

PURUSHAMEDHA

"So it's worth it?" I asked?

"Well, that depends on what you think is worthwhile in this universe. I could do the ritual and make a lot of money, but I don't want money. I just want to spend my days here, chant some rounds, please Lord Sankarsana, and then go down to Patala when all is said and done."

He smiled gently, and he patted me again on the shoulder, and ushered me outside. "Go do your chores," he said, "and try to not think about this too much. It will only distract you from Krsna."

And he was right, of course, and in time it seemed less shocking. But Krsna likes to shock us, He wants to shock us, to help us break free of this world of maya, and to get back in touch with Him, no matter what the cost.

PURUSHAMEDHA

PURUSHAMEDHA

RUDRA DAS GOSWAMI

PURUSHAMEDHA

CREDITS: All images used herein are courtesy of Wikimedia Commons, with the exception of several private photos submitted by the author. Quotations throughout this book from Bhaktivedanta editions (e.g. *Bhagavad Gita* and *Srimad Bhagavatam*) are taken from the website <vedabase.com>, and used under Fair Use copyright law. This use in no way suggests any endorsement from BBT or connection to the BBT. These links are valid at the time of writing, but no guarantee can be made of their stability.

p.3 https://upload.wikimedia.org/wikipedia/commons/2/2a/The_three-headed_rakshasa_Trishiras_sits_in_-lalitasana_on_a_throne_facing_a_-fire_altar_in_which_a_severed_head_is_burning.jpg

p. 39 - https://upload.wikimedia.org/wikipedia/commons/f/f9/Kumbha-karna_Kecak.jpg

P.68 https://agniveerfan.files.wordpress.com/2011/11/animal-sacrifice-by-hindus.jpg

p.84 https://upload.wikimedia.org/wikipedia/commons/9/91/Yajna1.jpg

P. 99 https://upload.wikimedia.org/wikipedia/commons/b/bf/Adi_-Sesha_with_Sivalinga.JPG

p. 114 https://upload.wikimedia.org/wikipedia/commons/d/dc/Shiva_-Statue_Murdeshwara_Temple.jpg

p.118 https://upload.wikimedia.org/wikipedia/commons/e/e1/Vishnu_-Yagna_Kunda.jpg

p.153 https://upload.wikimedia.org/wikipedia/commons/2/23/Asvam-edha_ramayana.JPG

PURUSHAMEDHA

Cover Image: Original image by Joe deSousa, taken from <Flikr.com>. Image listed as Public Domain photo.

Hare Krsna mantra (multiple pages) - https://upload.wikimedia.org/wikipedia/common s/e/e4/Mahamantra.gif

www.ingramcontent.com/pod-product-compliance
Lightning Source LLC
Chambersburg PA
CBHW060156050426
42446CB00013B/2859